Now & Then OMAN

In August 1971, His Majesty Sultan Qaboos stepped down from the Fokker F27 onto Bait Al Falaj airstrip for the first time as the new Sultan. During his first 31 years as Ruler, Sultan Qaboos has led his country through a remarkable transformation.

"Take what you need from nature and no more"
H.M. Sultan Qaboos bin Said Al-Said

Our Earth Series
Volume VIII
By John J. Nowell *LRPS FRGS*

Foreword

The Sultanate of Oman situated on the southeast corner of the Arabian Peninsula has its roots deep in history. Evidence of Oman once known as 'Magan' can be traced back to the 3rd Millennium BC. It is an unforgettable country with an awesome physical presence, many lively traditions, a rich cultural heritage and hospitable friendly people. Oman's mountain ranges and diverse landscape are believed to have taken over 800 million years to develop; it is considered to be the best natural geological museum in the world. There are deserts where sand dunes form rippled mountains that are constantly forming and re-forming, lush oases where mud brick villages are shaded by lofty palm groves; beautiful untouched beaches where rare turtles lay their eggs; and, in the southern region of Dhofar, known as the Land of Frankincense, there is a unique monsoon climate where you can find green mountains, camels and coconuts in abundance. On the 23rd July 1970, His Majesty Sultan Qaboos bin Said became our Sultan continuing the line of the longest reigning dynasty in the region. At that time our country, was known as 'Muscat and Oman' and had remained unchanged for hundreds of years. Little was known of our country in the outside world and only a small number of roads, hospitals and schools existed. After his Accession HM Sultan Qaboos bin Said quickly made use of the newly discovered oil to develop and unify our country and open her doors to the outside world. In 1970, our Sultan unified the nation and her people by declaring that henceforth Muscat and Oman would be known as the Sultanate of Oman. He also welcomed all those Omanis living abroad to return and support this new page in Omani history. Our Sultan began to build the foundations and infrastructure of a modern forward-looking country. He soon established a new government and diplomatic relations. Vast networks of new roads were introduced allowing access to even remote areas once difficult to reach. Schools, hospitals, clinics, public housing schemes, electricity and telecommunications systems were established. International airports and seaports were created and developed. As a result, trade and industry increased and flourished, and Oman has prospered into a nation that successfully combines tradition with modernity. Today, we welcome global tourism and business. Bold, new, ambitious plans to build more hotel resorts are underway. New ports and free zones are being introduced to encourage global players to establish their business in Oman. Such ventures will provide employment for our newly educated Omani youth. It is difficult to explain this development to people who have not actually witnessed the renaissance of our country, and to show how rapidly our country grew and continues to grow. However, the photographs within the pages of this book, graphically demonstrate this development. They allow the reader to step back in time and experience the changing face of our proud nation. With the advent of the new millennium, it is interesting to consider this visual assessment of these dramatic changes that have occurred during the last 31 years in the Sultanate of Oman under the wise leadership of His Majesty Sultan Qaboos.

Mohammad Al Zubair
Advisor to HM The Sultan for Economic Planning Affairs,
Founder of Bait Al Zubair Museum, Muscat.
The Sultanate of Oman.

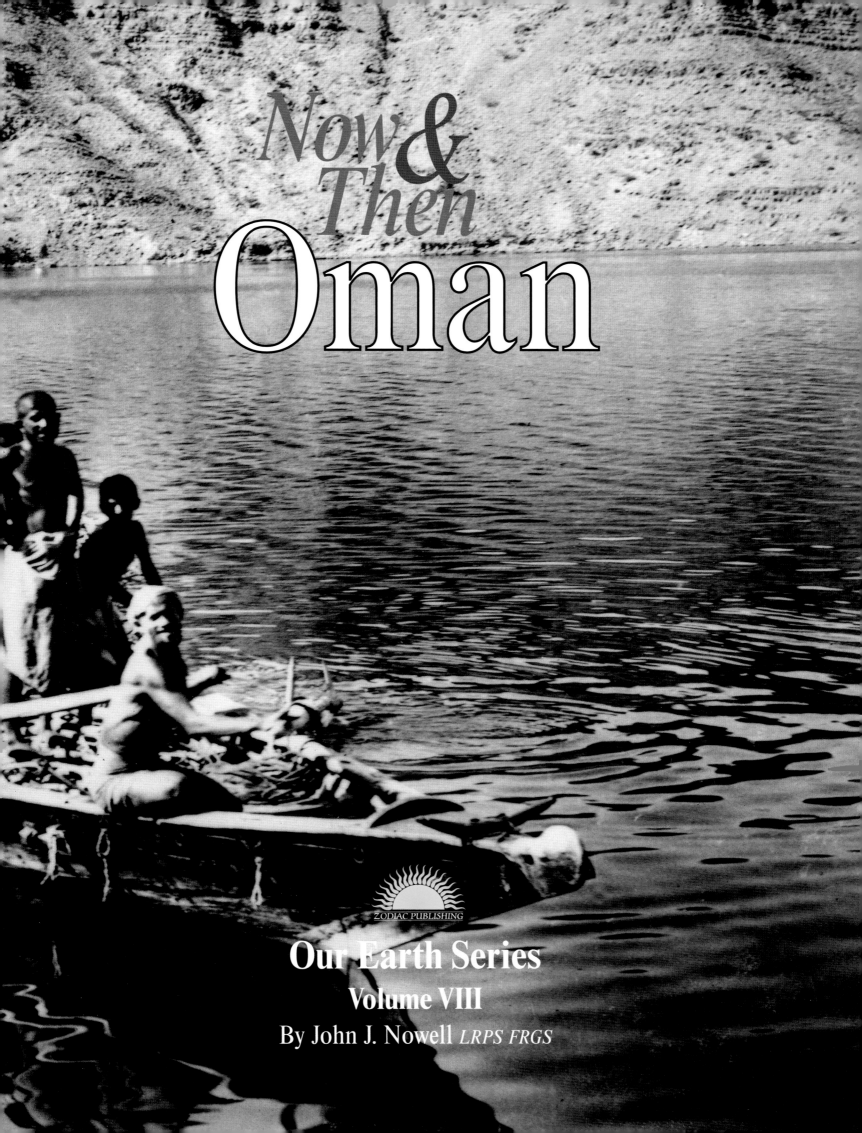

Now & Then
Oman

ZODIAC PUBLISHING

Our Earth Series
Volume VIII
By John J. Nowell *LRPS FRGS*

Published by Zodiac Publishing, Dubai.

Zodiac Publishing, Registered Office
P.O.Box 170, Churchill Buildings
Grand Turk, Turks & Caicos Islands

Zodiac Publishing, Dubai
PO Box 35121, Dubai, UAE
Tel: 0971 4 - 2826966 Fax: 0971 4 - 2826882
e-mail: zodiacpublishing@hotmail.com

First published 2001.

Copyright: John J. Nowell 2001.

Other books in the series:

  Now & Then The Emirates
  Now & Then Bahrain
  Now & Then Abu Dhabi
  Now & Then Dubai

*A Day Above Oman
*A Day Above The Emirates
 A Day Above Yemen
 A Day Above Jiddah Island
* These books are published by Motivate Publishing

ISBN 0 - 9533033-5-7

British Library Cataloguing - in - Publication Data.
A catalogue record for this book is available
from the British Library.

Design by Nick Crawley of Zodiac Publishing.
Separations & Printing by Emirates Printing Press, Dubai.
"Now & Then" is a Zodiac Publishing registered trademark.

Contents

Page P6-7:
Muttrah Harbour. This aerial photograph was taken by the Royal Air Force some time after the Second World War. At the lower left is Muttrah fort and behind, in the center of the photograph is the bulk of the main souq of Muttrah with buildings actually built on the waters edge. Dhows are at anchor in the yards and tracks lead away to the top of the picture towards Wadi Kabir and the Ruwi valley. Today the capital city of Muscat stretches from Seeb to Quriyat and the old souq of Muttrah is separated from the sea by an elegant Corniche.

Page P8-9:
The Shabab Oman sail training ship has the unique distinction of having won the Cutty Sark award twice. Since the inception of the Sail Training Association, no other nation in the world has won this trophy for a second time. This beautiful vessel is not only a sail training ship but also performs a much broader role of that of a roving ambassador for the Sultanate of Oman, to remind the world of the maritime heritage of Oman. The ship has undertaken numerous international voyages visiting Japan, Europe and the United States.

Page 10-11:
Records as early as the seventh century AD point to the considerable reputation of Oman's warriors. A document dated 678 AD refers to the existence of a mercenary force of 3,000 Omani warriors serving with the forces of Al Muhallab bin Abi Safra at Basra. A large proportion of troops in this army were mounted and the process of war and conquest led to the improvement of Arabian equestrian bloodlines. The animals brought back to Oman from Basra, were of better stock than those that had left. The Indian Army purchased horses from Oman as early as the year 950 AD, a commercial agreement that continued until the 1930s!

Introduction

OMAN IS AN OLD LAND. ROCK STRATA IN THE DHOFAR AREA NEAR MIRBAT HAVE BEEN DATED BACK to 800 million years ago. During a recent archaeological expedition, made by a team from Sultan Qaboos University, the remains of 65 million year old dinosaurs were found. The remains appear to be that of the carnivorous Therapods and the herbivore Sauropods. The Sauropods were giant, four legged, long necked creatures that roamed the earth in the late Cretaceous period, some 65 – 100 million years ago. During the same period the remains of the forests were laid down as formations that eventually formed the oil reserves that we rely on today.

The rocks of Oman contain evidence of a remarkable journey. Millions of years ago, as fires raged and rocks melted deep within the earth's core, the great continent of Gondwana split apart and the continents, as we know them now, took their initial shape. The continents then drifted over the surface of the mantle until they reached their present positions. The rocks of Oman record over 800 million years of geological history, showing that Oman has moved between sub polar latitudes and its present tropical position several times. This caused huge changes in the climate and rock deposits. Over 730 million years ago plate movements squeezed together sediment and igneous rocks to create the continental plate that lies beneath Arabia. 700 million years ago, Oman was land punctuated by frequent volcanic eruptions that sent large amounts of ash into the air. When the ash settled, it formed layers that then became rock. 600 million years ago, the first life forms existed in the shallow seas that covered Arabia and Oman. 560 million years ago, the Arabian Plate had drifted northwards and was in tropical latitudes but by 300 million years ago, Oman was back in sub polar latitudes. The climate was very cold and ice sheets and glaciers covered the land. 280 million years ago, as the Arabian Plate moved towards warmer latitudes, the climate warmed up and the ice sheets melted. Winding rivers flowed slowly across the plains with large trees growing on their banks. Some tree trunks were trapped in the river sediments and fossilized. 70 million years ago a warm, shallow sea covered Oman, but this gradually retreated and the present day conditions evolved.

The Sultanate of Oman occupies the southeastern corner of the Arabian Peninsula and is located between latitudes 16 40' and 26 20' north and longitudes 51 50' and 59 40' East. The coastline extends 1,700 kilometres from the Strait of Hormuz in the north to the borders of the Republic of Yemen and overlooks three seas - the Arabian Gulf, the Gulf of Oman and the Arabian Sea. The Sultanate of Oman borders Saudi Arabia and the United Arab Emirates in the West; the Republic of Yemen in the South; the Strait of Hormuz in the North and the Arabian Sea in the East. The total land area is approximately 309,500 sq. kms; it is the third largest country in the Arabian Peninsula. Oman has a variety of topographical features consisting of plains, wadis and mountains. The most important area, the coastal plain, represents about 3% of the total land area and is the centre of agriculture. The mountain ranges occupy about 15%. The Hajar range runs from Musandam in the North to Ras al-Hadd, the extreme limit of the Arabian Peninsula. In the South, the Qara range is affected by the monsoon, which brings unique weather conditions and creates a special environment in Dhofar. The remaining area, which occupies 82% of the country, is mainly sand and gravel desert including part of the Empty Quarter, the largest desert in Arabia. The climate differs from one area to

another: it is hot and humid in the coastal areas in summer and warm and dry in winter; it is hot and dry in the Interior with the exception of the higher mountains which enjoy a moderate climate throughout the year. Rainfall is generally light and irregular although heavy rains and thunderstorms can cause severe flooding. In the south, the Dhofar region has a moderate climate and the pattern of rainfall is more predictable with heavy monsoon rains occurring regularly between May and September. The main town is Salalah, which lies on the fertile coastal plain where the principal occupations are fishing and agriculture. Raysut, to the West of Salalah, is Oman's second port and the location for a new industrial area. The Dhofar Mountains, with their unique climate, provide valuable pasture for cattle, camels and goats. Offshore, the Halaniyat Islands support a small fishing community. Musandam is a spectacular area with mountains rising up to 1,800 metres and falling precipitately into the sea, a combination that once formed an almost impenetrable barrier. It is now linked with the rest of Oman by a modern road network. The main centres are Khasab and Bukha and the major commercial activity is fishing.

The arrival of man in the area was a relatively recent happening. To grasp the significance of the timescale, consider the following analogy. If the entire life of the Earth were reduced to just one year, the starting point of the Earth would be 1st January. By 1st June, the first living form would have appeared. In October, the dinosaurs would have come and gone. On the 31st December, at 2300 hrs, the first humans appeared. In the countdown to midnight, with forty seconds to go, the art of writing started, and the first human reached Oman. The present dynasty of Oman occupied the final second and this book covers a fraction of that final second.

Little is known about Oman's pre-Islamic past but it is clear from recent archaeological discoveries and research that early civilisations existed at least 6000 years ago. Sumerian tablets refer to a country named "Magan" as a source of copper. It seems certain that they referred to Oman. Evidence from excavations near Sohar shows that the copper mining and smelting industry was well developed by the year 2000 BC. Frankincense from Dhofar, which was so important in the social and religious life of ancient peoples, provides evidence of the existence of an early trading community. It is also clear that there were farming and fishing settlements in the earliest times. The ancestors of present day Omanis are believed to have arrived in two waves of migration over a number of years, the first from the Yemen and the second from northern Arabia, at a period in history when the Persians occupied various parts of the country.

The call of the Prophet Mohammed (PBUH) to the Omanis to embrace Islam altered the course of their history. It was in about 630 AD that Amir Ibn al-As arrived in Oman bearing a letter from the Prophet to Abd and Jaifar, the two sons of al-Julanda, who jointly ruled Oman. The first Ibadhi Imam, Julanda bin Mas'ud, was elected in 751 AD but he died in battle and it was not until 801 AD, after a period of turmoil, that Warith bin Kaab was elected. There then followed a period of peace, stability and prosperity lasting more than three hundred years. Maritime trade flourished and Sohar became the greatest seaport in the Islamic world. As they travelled and traded, the Omanis spread the message of Islam, as well as Arab culture and language, their influence reaching as far as China.

In the early 16th century, the Portuguese, under Vasco de Gama, discovered the sea route round the Cape of Good Hope to India. They occupied Muscat for a century and a half in order to dominate the sea trade which had until then been an Arab monopoly. The Portuguese were expelled from Muscat in 1650 by Sultan bin Saif al-Yarubi. Since the expulsion of the Portuguese no other foreign power has ever occupied Oman, apart from a brief period when the Persians made a partial occupation. The Ya'aruba Imams introduced a period of renaissance in Oman and made fortunes both at home and abroad, uniting the country and bringing stability and prosperity. It was under the Ya'aruba dynasty that many of the imposing castles and beautiful buildings, such as the recently restored fort at Nizwa and the Palace at Jabrin, were built. On the death in 1718 of the Imam, Sultan bin Saif II, civil war broke out over the election of his successor. Persian troops occupied Muttrah and Muscat but failed to take Sohar, which was defended, by Ahmad bin Said, who eventually defeated the Persians.

In 1744 Ahmad bin Said, a man of outstanding personality and courage, was elected Imam. He faced numerous difficulties in reconciling the rival factions that existed after the civil war. Nevertheless, he managed to build the Omani navy into a formidable power, personally leading expeditions against pirates and driving the Persians out of Basra. When he died in 1783, his son Said was elected Imam but was replaced by his son Hamad, who had been de facto ruler in Muscat. Hamad died suddenly in 1792 and his uncle, Sayyid Sultan bin Ahmed, assumed power until his death in 1804. Sayyid Sultan was succeeded by his son, Sayyid Said bin Sultan, who consolidated his father's achievements at home and abroad from 1804-1856. It was in this period that Oman reached its zenith as a regional power with possessions on both sides of the Gulf and in East Africa. Sayyid Said concentrated on developing his country's economy and commerce. He made Zanzibar his second capital and concluded agreements with the European powers, as well as sending a special envoy to the United States, making Oman the first Arab state to establish diplomatic relations with that country. Thereafter, however, there followed a period of decline and at the time of the First World War, Oman's share of international commercial activities was very limited. Indeed, Oman remained largely isolated from the rest of the world until, in 1970, His Majesty Sultan Qaboos came to power.

His Majesty Sultan Qaboos was born in Salalah, in Dhofar, on the 18th of November 1940. He is the only son of the late Sultan Said bin Taimur and is eighth in the direct line of the al Busaidi dynasty. The dynasty was founded in 1744 by Imam Ahmad bin Said. His Majesty spent his youth in Salalah where he received a traditional education. At the age of 16, his father sent him to a private educational establishment in England. In 1960 he entered the Royal Military Academy at Sandhurst as an officer cadet. Having passed out of Sandhurst, he joined a British infantry battalion on operational duty in Germany for one year and also held a staff appointment with the British Army. After his military service His Majesty studied local government in England and went on a world tour before returning home. The next six years were spent in Salalah studying Islam and the history of his country and people.

On the abdication of his father and his own accession on 23rd July 1970, the

Renaissance of Oman began. His Majesty arrived in Muscat on the 9th August 1970 where he made the first of many speeches setting out his vision for his people and his country. He declared that the country would have a new flag and that it would no longer be called 'Muscat and Oman' but unified as the Sultanate of Oman. Restrictions on freedom of movement were lifted and Omanis who had left the country were invited to return to take part in the challenge that lay ahead. Due to the complete absence of infrastructure in 1970, the task facing His Majesty was a formidable one. Although Oman had received oil revenues for three years, very little development had been implemented. Not only was the country extremely backward in health, education, housing and communications, but to add to these difficulties a full-scale local war was being fought in Dhofar, in the south of the country, against a communist insurgency, with a small, inadequately equipped army Thanks to his inspired and dedicated leadership, Oman has become an oasis of prosperity and stability in a troubled world. Today, after over thirty years of outstanding achievements, His Majesty is seeking a change of direction for his country in keeping with the economic demands of the 21st century and the aspirations of his people. Another fundamental transformation in Oman's fortunes is taking place with the private sector replacing the public sector as the vehicle for progress and prosperity.

His Majesty has always been concerned with the basic rights and duties of the Omani citizen. In 1996, a Royal Decree promulgated the Basic Statute of the State. It consists of seven chapters and 81 articles, dealing with every aspect of the State apparatus and fundamental human rights. The Basic Statute guarantees the equality of all citizens before the law, freedom of religion, freedom of speech, a free press; the right to a fair trial and the right to form nationally based associations. It lays down a legal framework for all future legislation and provides for the succession. Article Five states that the system of government is 'Royal' and hereditary in the male descendants of Sayyid Turki bin Said bin Sultan (the great-great-grandfather of His Majesty) and that the successor to the throne shall be a Muslim, of sound mind, and the legitimate son of Omani Muslim parentage. The following article stipulates that the Ruling Family Council will choose the successor within three days of the throne falling vacant. If the Ruling Family Council cannot agree on the choice of successor, the Defence Council shall confirm the appointment of the person designated by the Sultan in his letter to the Ruling Family Council.

Relations have also been strengthened with countries throughout the world and His Majesty continues to lead the development of the political structure and the infrastructure of Oman. In a reign spanning more than 3 decades, Sultan Qaboos has seen Oman develop from an isolated country to become a unique example of a modern state. His personal values were summed up in a speech made to young officers at a passing-out parade, His Majesty said of his own military training: "*I know that the values that I absorbed have remained with me forever afterwards. I learned that discipline is not just something one imposes on others: it is something that one has, above all, to apply to oneself if one is to be a worthy leader of men. I learned also the true meaning of service: that it is to give and not to expect to receive: that it is the team and not oneself that matters. I learned that with responsibility comes obligation*".

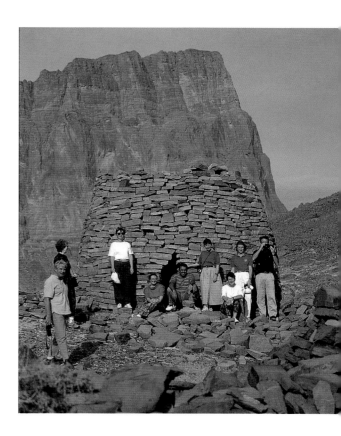

Chapter 1
The History of Oman

THE OLDEST EVIDENCE OF HUMAN SETTLEMENT IN THE REGION DATES from 5000 years ago. A large number of tower tombs of the "Umm Al Nar" period are distributed all over Oman. The world came to know about the tombs situated above Tiwi, by sheer chance. One afternoon, I had flown the helicopter to Sur on a beautiful late afternoon following the northern coastline of Oman. At Sur we landed and disembarked our VIP passengers. Normally, we wouldn't fly over the mountains, due to the possibility of turbulence but as it was very calm I decided to fly home the direct way through the mountains. Only ten minutes after take off, we were at 5000 feet at the same height as the mountain tops, flying through the high valleys. Silhouetted against the setting sun, I saw a line of "pimples" on a high plateau. My curiosity at such perfection was aroused and I turned and flew towards them. At

short range, it became clear that here was a collection of beautiful tower tombs. I landed, shut the helicopter and we got out to take a closer look. The air was very still and, apart form the metal tinkling of the cooling engines, it was very quiet. One of the tombs had a small opening and I crawled inside but found the tomb totally empty. Outside again, I took several photographs and later showed them to His Majesty who asked me to send them to The Ministry of Heritage. After the photographs were published in my first book "A Day Above Oman", Paul Yule, a German archaeologist, contacted me. Together, in a 4-wheel drive, on loan from Zubair Tours, we struggled for two days to reach the tombs I had photographed. Paul issued an international press release and the enclosed cutting appeared on the front page of The Times on 2nd December 1991.

WITH THE ARRIVAL OF ISLAM IN **640 AD**, A NEW order was established throughout Oman. The Sun's path across the heaven was used to regulate times of prayer. Muslims observe five daily prayers or *Salat*, the most important duty of worship in Islam, second only to the testimony of faith, the *Shahada*: dawn prayers (*Al Fajr*) take place at first light; noon prayers (*Al Dhuuor*) are performed when the sun is in the middle of the sky, afternoon prayers (*Al Asr*) when the shadow is the same length as an object, at sunset, it is time for *Al Mahgieb*, *Al Isha* marks the end of evening twilight.

"Qalhat has many fine bazaars and a very beautiful mosque, the walls are tiled with qashani tiles which resemble enamel. It stands on an eminence overlooking the sea and anchorage and was built by a holy woman, Bibi Maryam. The inhabitants are traders and live entirely on what comes to them from the Indian Ocean. Whenever a vessel arrives at the town they show the greatest joy."

Ibn Battuta c1368

"Kalhat [sic] is a fine city on the sea coast 600 miles north-west of Dhofar. No corn is grown here, but it is imported by sea from other places. This city has a good port, much frequented by merchant ships from India. They find a ready market here for their wares, since it is a centre from which spices and other goods are carried to various inland cities and towns. Many fine warhorses are exported from here to India, to the great gain of the merchants. The people of this country live on dates and salt fish, of which they enjoy abundant supplies. But admittedly there are some among them, men of wealth and consequence, who eat foods of better quality."

Marco Polo, c 1292

Inset is a photograph of a mud brick tower house in the Buraimi Oasis. This photograph was taken in 1954 from a Hawker Hunter fighter reconnaissance aircraft.

IN 1494, POPE ALEXANDER VI DIVIDED THE unexplored portions of the planet, by the Treaty of Tordesillas, between the rival interests of Spain and Portugal. The Treaty drew a line of longitude a hundred leagues west of the Azores, granting Spain everything west of it and Portugal everything to the east. At the time the earth was considered to be flat and so in 1543 Spanish galleons could be found claiming the Philippines, having sailed west across the Pacific from the New World. The domination of Portuguese forces throughout the Indian Ocean tends to exalt the early Portuguese explorers as having 'discovered' much of the Indian Ocean as shown on this contemporary map. This conveniently ignores the existing regional trade, much of it conducted over astonishing distances in perilous circumstances.

In ancient times, Herodutus reported that cinnamon came from African swamps guarded by bats, and was used by giant birds for their nests. Cinnamon actually came from Indonesia 4,000 miles away across the Indian Ocean. Double outrigger canoes traded their spices along the Cinnamon Route that stretched from Indonesia to the islands of Madagascar and Zanzibar off the east coast of Africa. The Chinese navy dominated the Arabian Sea at the time. The prodigious feats of the Grand Admiral Zheng He of China, the so-called 'Three Jewelled Eunuch', led to the appearance at Court in Peking in 1414 of a giraffe captured at Malindi in East Africa. (This was whilst the much-vaunted 'Henry the Navigator' of Portugal was still struggling to get his ships down the coast of North West Africa). In Malindi, near to the spot where the giraffe was led on board an ocean going junk sailing for China, an unremarkable stone pillar, a *padrao*, can still be found, erected by Portuguese sailors to commemorate the place from which, a year earlier, they had set off across the Indian Ocean to become the first Europeans to sail all the way to India. In 1498, the Portuguese fleet, led by the nobleman Vasco da Gama, reached Calicut, a rich trading city on the

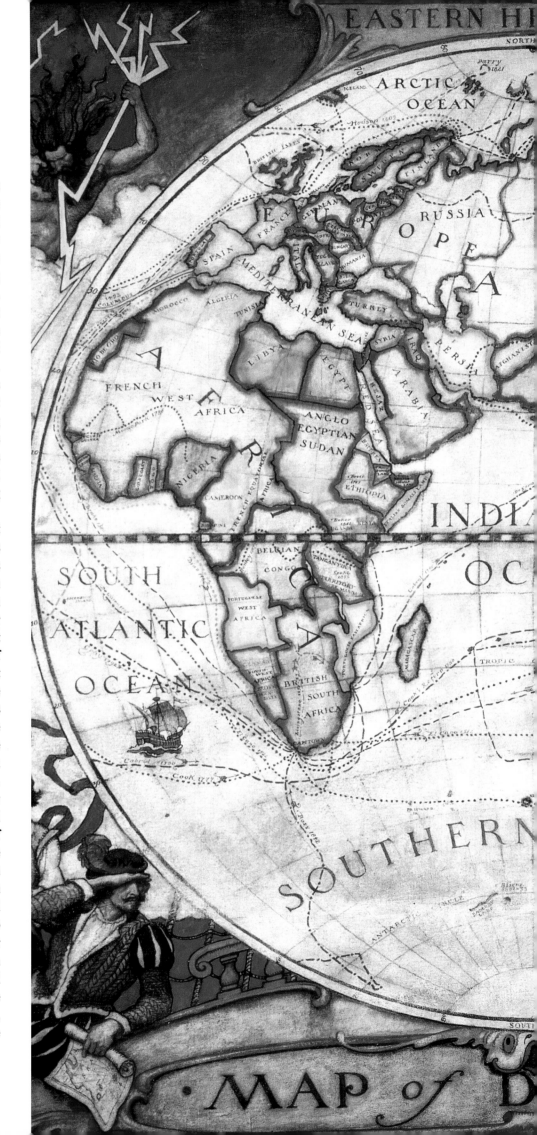

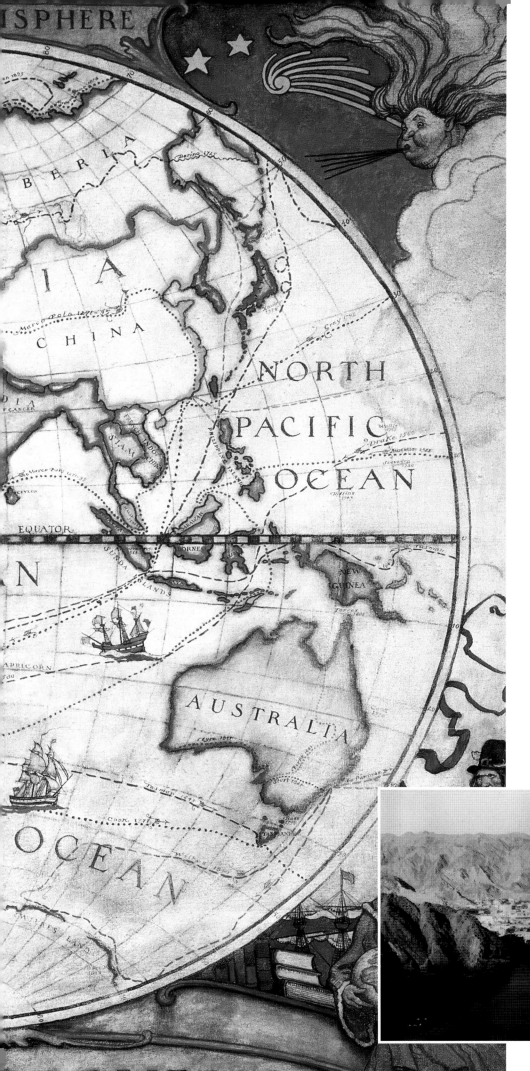

southwest coast of India. The Portuguese, led by Alfonso de Albuquerque, captured Muscat in 1507. In his notes Albuquerque recorded that both Qalhat and Sohar were well-established ports, frequently shipping livestock, cattle and horses to India. He went on to reveal that in Sohar he saw a native and well-disciplined cavalry regiment of some 500 troops and horses. The horses were kept in well-designed stables and wore a form of chain mail armour. Sohar at that time appears to have been the main horse breeding area although the plain of Quriyat, near Sur, were also an important breeding centre, with horses grazing throughout the area.

English seafarers such as Sir Francis Drake made full use of their license, granted by Queen Elizabeth 1 of England, to plunder the Portuguese and Spanish ships, and in a few years learnt as much about world navigation as it had taken Spain and Portugal a hundred years to acquire. The capture, in 1592, of a Portuguese ship loaded with a rich cargo of jewels, spices, porcelain, silks and other luxuries from the East Indies caused a sensation when it docked at Dartmouth, as did the discovery on board of a register of the 'Government and Trade of the Portuguese in the East Indies'. These discoveries paved the way for the establishment of the East India Company.

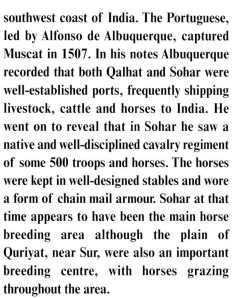

ON 31ST DECEMBER 1600, ELIZABETH I OF ENGLAND PUT HER SIGNATURE to the Royal Charter which gave birth to the 'Governor and Company of Merchants trading into the East Indies', known as the ' East India Company', which legalized the ambitions of the original subscribers, 218 merchants and tradesmen of the City of London. Although the Queen died only two years after granting the Company its Charter, it was a supremely Elizabethan invention, the culmination of an age, which saw England, transformed from a second-rate, semi-piratical nation to a cultured, ambitious and revolutionary first-rank European power. The earlier 'exclusive' trading rights asserted by the Spanish and the defiant English treated Portuguese in the East with little respect.

The First Voyage of the Company (each fleet, separately funded, was called a 'Voyage') set out in February 1601 under Captain James Lancaster. His flagship was the *Dragon*, the other vessels the *Hector*, the *Susan* and the *Ascension*. The fleet carried Sterling 28, 472 of bullion for purchases, and goods worth a further Sterling 6,860, including wrought iron, crockery, pistols and spectacles. Lancaster knew enough about scurvy: the plague of English sailors at that time, to take lemon juice aboard to provide his crew with necessary vitamin C but the captains of the other ships took the decision not to adopt this precaution. As a result, Lancaster's crew enjoyed full possession of their teeth all the way to the Cape, whilst many of the men in other ships parted company with theirs, and 105 lost their lives altogether. (The use of lemon or limejuice, which seemed so clearly efficacious, surprisingly remained the matter of a captain's whim for years to come.) Ships from England called regularly at Muscat to make an essential purchase of dried limes. English sailors eventually became universally known as "limeys" because of their consumption of limes.

BY THE 1800S, OMAN ATTRACTED AN increasing number of visitors. Lt Col Samuel Miles was one of the first to travel inland and visit Nizwa;

"The sheikh told me that the textile and embroidery industries of Nezwa [sic], once so famous and extensive, had entirely disappeared. After breakfast I took a walk through the town and environs to make myself acquainted with them, and found them so extensive that they required some time to realize the varied aspect of the whole. The city is unwalled, and the space it covers is a medley of walled quarters, intermingled with groves of graceful palms, fruit orchards, odorous gardens, and running streams, which, backed and sheltered by the grand mountains above them, present a remarkable picture of wild, natural scenery combined with luxuriant fertility and the evidence of human prosperity...

I visited more than once the busy and thriving bazaars, watching the coppersmiths, braziers, dyers and others. Among the artisans are makers of camel-saddles, potters, silversmiths, cobblers, cameleen weavers, carpenters, makers of hulwa – the national sweetmeat, for which Nezwa is famous, as it has a different flavour from that of Mascat, and is largely exported – blacksmiths, sugar or treacle makers, masons, mat weavers and others. But the most noteworthy part of the bazaar, which is only shaded from the sun by strips of matting here and there, and is not particularly clean, is the copper market, which though inviting by the quaintness of is ware, is repellent from the incessant noise and deafening din of the hammering going on."

Lieutenant-Colonel Samuel Miles, 1884

For centuries, Omani people have fearlessly defended their faith, their families, their homes and lands armed first with lance and sword and later with rifles. The very rare photograph, taken in 1911, shows the son of Sultan Sayyid Faisal Bin Turki, Sayyid Taimur Bin Faisal, mounted on an Arab stallion and armed with a Martini Henry rifle and sword.

Sultan Qaboos, as a young man completed the British Army course at the Royal Military College at Sandhurst. Time has moved on and, whilst the same courageous spirit continues to live in the heart of every Omani, today's modern Royal Army of Oman is equipped with the latest, high technology, armoured fighting vehicles.

For the past thirty years the British company, Alvis Vehicles Limited, who also support the RAO in its own training, maintenance and logistics operations, has supplied many of these vehicles. Pictured here is the new Desert Piranha armoured vehicle, a state of the art-armoured personnel carrier made by Alvis. The highly mobile Desert Piranha has been specially adapted to operate in extreme environments. The Royal Army of Oman is a fine example of a modern, defensive force, regularly participating in international defence exercises and providing a stable and secure influence in the region.

HER MAJESTY QUEEN ELISABETH II, acompanied by the Duke of Edinburgh, are welcomed by His Majesty Sultan Qaboos. 100 years earlier, another visitor to the palace said… "We proceeded to His Highness the Sayyid's palace…going up and down a number of narrow streets, or rather lanes, for there is not a genuine street in all Muscat… We found ourselves in a sort of courtyard, around which was built the palace, a very unpretentious, two-storeyed edifice. To our left, close to the gateway, was a good-sized room, in which reclined a splendid African lion; the front of the lion's parlour was formed of iron bars similar to those which protect the plate glass of jewellers' shops in London at night. …In the centre of the courtyard a leopard occupied a cage; on our right were eight or ten Arab mares, some of which were evidently of considerable value, and the horse-keepers lay about on the pavement."

Gratton Geary, Editor of The Times of India, March 1878

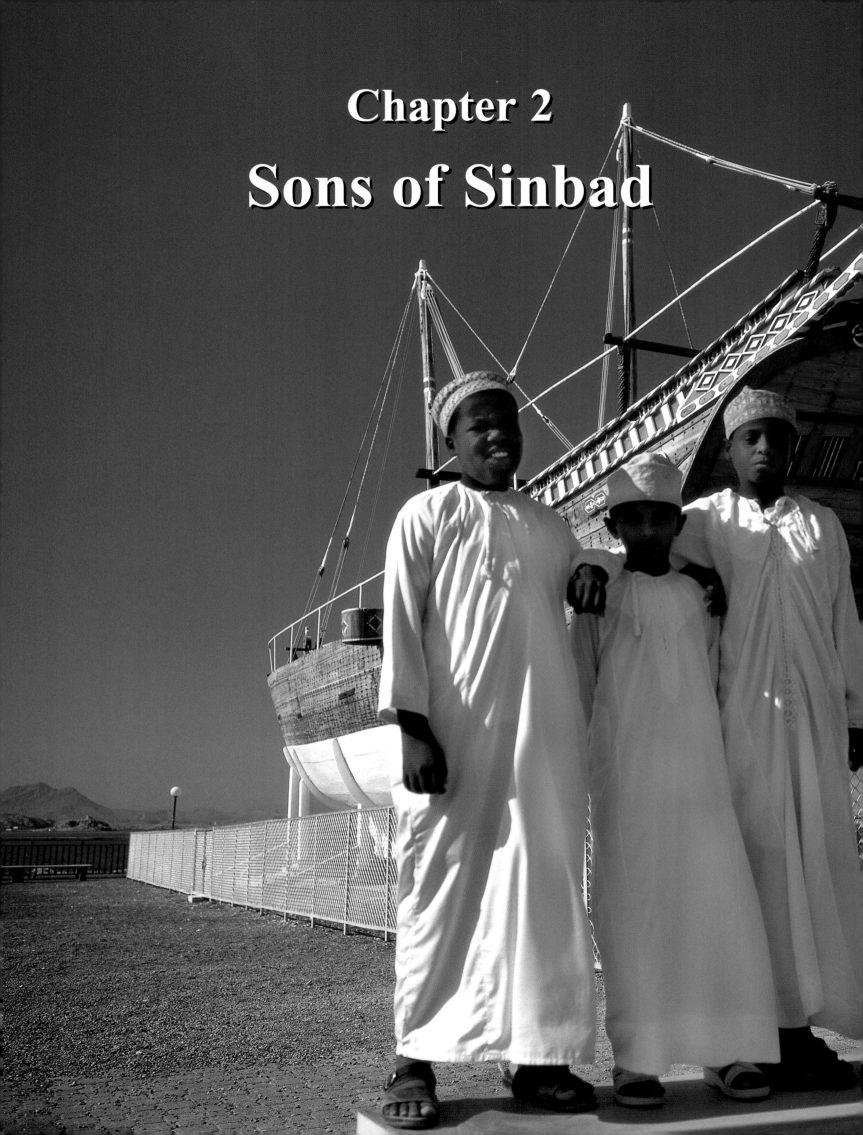

Chapter 2
Sons of Sinbad

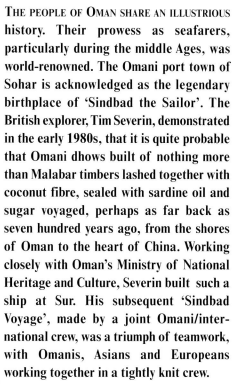

THE PEOPLE OF OMAN SHARE AN ILLUSTRIOUS history. Their prowess as seafarers, particularly during the middle Ages, was world-renowned. The Omani port town of Sohar is acknowledged as the legendary birthplace of 'Sindbad the Sailor'. The British explorer, Tim Severin, demonstrated in the early 1980s, that it is quite probable that Omani dhows built of nothing more than Malabar timbers lashed together with coconut fibre, sealed with sardine oil and sugar voyaged, perhaps as far back as seven hundred years ago, from the shores of Oman to the heart of China. Working closely with Oman's Ministry of National Heritage and Culture, Severin built such a ship at Sur. His subsequent 'Sindbad Voyage', made by a joint Omani/international crew, was a triumph of teamwork, with Omanis, Asians and Europeans working together in a tightly knit crew.

OMANI SAILORS DEVELOPED THE ART OF navigation many centuries ago. Navigation depended on knowledge of the stars and early sailors contributed to a rich store of astronomical information – about 48 stars are still identified by their Arabic names. The famous 15th century sailor, Ahmed Bin Majed, sometimes known as 'Sindbad the Sailor', not only wrote books on navigation, but also wrote poetry about the movements of the stars. Out of the thousands of stars visible to the naked eye, only 48 are used for navigation. These stars are universally known by their Arabic names – Al Yah the north, Al Quoth the South, Mutlan the east, Al Maghib the West, Ayoon Maghib the northwest and Aqurab Maghib the southwest. Two stars,

Sohail and Al Hamarin, guided dhows travelling from Oman to Africa. Halfway across, another star Al Aqurab brought vessels safely to port in Zanzibar. "Allah has said: "We have determined the different positions of the moon throughout the month, then she returns like the old and withered, lower part of a date stalk" (The Quran - The Muslim calendar follows the lunar year (12 months – 355 days). The beginning of the month is marked by the first appearance of the crescent moon and the different phases of the moon were linked to various events and traditions; the best time to travel in the desert used to be between the 5th and 20th night of the lunar month, the time when the moon was at its brightest.

MUCH OF THE DHOW TRADE DEVELOPED WHEN there was surplus produce to export. Astronomy played an important part in traditional Omani agriculture. Water was always the most vital ingredient and legend tells us that;"One Day, the blessed Prophet Suleiman bin Da'ud, flying on his daily journey from Persepolis to Jerusalem, was blown off course by a strong wind. When he looked down, the blessed Prophet King Suleiman (Solomon), son of Da'ud (David) saw, in the strange landscape of Oman, a splendid castle. And he sent down his agents to investigate. They reported that an eagle lived there and that the only inhabitants of the land were Bedu. And the blessed Prophet Suleiman bin Da'ud commanded his agents to dig for water in the mountains, to produce a flaj, water channels, a thousand a day, and he stayed for ten days." The falaj delivered all the water used for drinking, cooking and washing. Underground channels, raised aqueducts and surface channels had to be constructed in extremely difficult and remote geographical areas. Once the Umm al falaj (the mother of the falaj) or water source was located, a gentle sloping channel would be constructed to let the water flow naturally to the settlement. In order to reduce water evaporation and to protect the falaj channel from flood damage, the main channel would usually take the form of a tunnel from the main water source to the first opening or *sharia* from which drinking water could be drawn. All the farmers in the areas surrounding the falaj depended on its water for irrigating their crops so several sub-channels split off from the main falaj channel, leading to the cultivated fields and orchards. These sub-channels were opened and closed according to an irrigation timetable established on the principles of a system known as *dawran*.

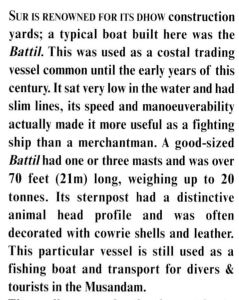

SUR IS RENOWNED FOR ITS DHOW construction yards; a typical boat built here was the *Battil*. This was used as a costal trading vessel common until the early years of this century. It sat very low in the water and had slim lines, its speed and manoeuverability actually made it more useful as a fighting ship than a merchantman. A good-sized *Battil* had one or three masts and was over 70 feet (21m) long, weighing up to 20 tonnes. Its sternpost had a distinctive animal head profile and was often decorated with cowrie shells and leather. This particular vessel is still used as a fishing boat and transport for divers & tourists in the Musandam.

These dhows made the long trip to Zanzibar, sometimes carrying passengers for a fare of US$2.50 for a 1,800-mile voyage. With the northeast winds to help, these dhows could travel up to 280 miles in a day. The crews waited in Zanzibar until the winds changed in April marking the start of the southwest monsoon followed by the run back to Arabia with a fair wind. The crews sailed south on the northeast monsoon, following the ripening of the Omani dates, and homeward on the southwest monsoon, a fair wind, up and down, one voyage a year.

THE TELEGRAPH STATION ON ELPHINSTONE ISLAND, deep in Khor Al Sha'm of the Musandam Peninsula, was constructed in 1864 when the British laid the first maritime telegraph cable through the Gulf. It ran from Karachi to Jask on the coast of Persia and onwards to Bushire and Fao via the Musandam Peninsula where there were two cable stations. One station at Ghubbat Ghazirah, known as Malcolm's Inlet and the other at Khor Al Sham (Elphinstone Inlet or Telegraph Island). The elegant vessel is the SS Earl Canning on a visit to the station in 1901. The island is also mentioned in the F540 – the operational record of No 203 Sqn. The record tells us that on 13th June 1933, one of the flying boats landed at the island to perform a medical evacuation of a telegraph operator who was taken back to Basra for treatment.

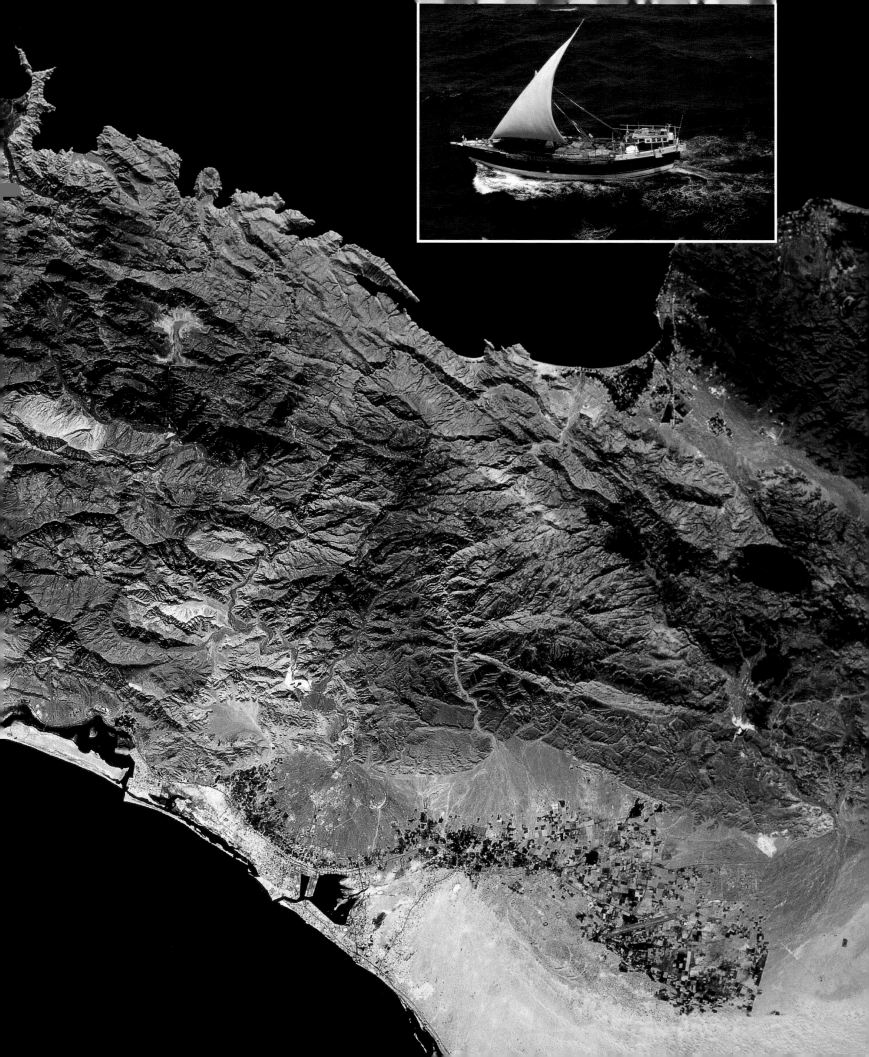

IN THE 10TH CENTURY, ONE OF THE MOST IMPORTANT ISLAMIC INVENTIONS WAS THE ASTROLOBE. FOR
several centuries, it was the most sophisticated scientific instrument in the world. The
original conception was probably made in Greece since the word astrolobe is actually
derived form the Greek word meaning "star finder". It is likely that the Arab astronomer,
Muhammad Musa al Khwarizmi, developed the astrolobe in the early 10th century. The
astrolobe is a globe that shows the positions of the sun and stars at any time of the day or
night throughout the year. Its primary use was as an aid to navigation. It enabled the
navigator to take star shots at specific times and hence fix his position on the surface of the
earth. Its secondary use was to calculate not only the times of sunrise and sunset, but also
the times of moonrise. The astrolobe was superseded in the 17th century by the sextant and
astronomical almanacs but astrolobes are still made today in India and can be found in local
souqs. Today, the Royal Yatch cruises the world using the latest navigational equipment

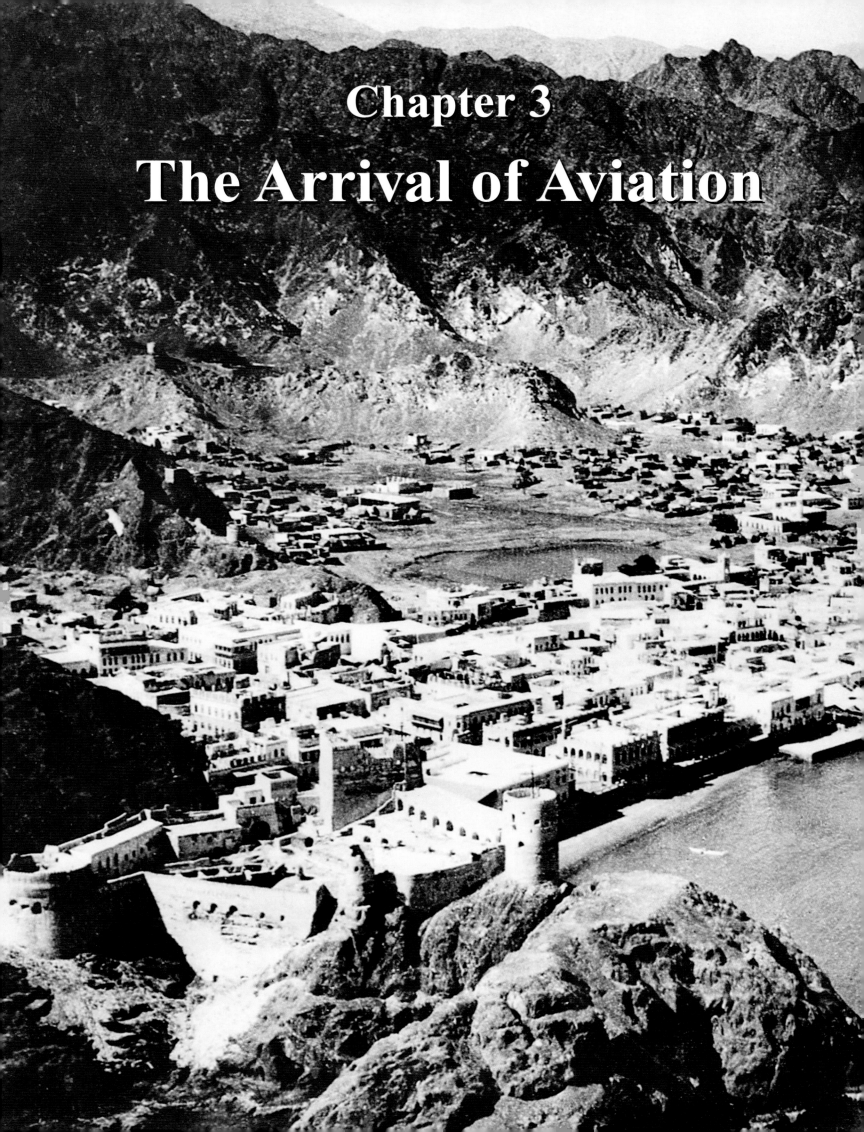

Chapter 3
The Arrival of Aviation

THE VERY FIRST AIRCRAFT TO LAND ON OMANI SOIL WERE TWO Westland Wapitis of 84 Squadron based at Shaibah near Basrah in Iraq. These aircraft were kitted out for long-range desert-patrol with a large fuel tanks bolted under the fuselages and a wind-driven auxilliary pumps at the pilot's right-hand. The aircraft sported the famous scorpion insignia, which became the badge for several RAF squadrons, associated with the Middle East. The Wapiti, an all-metal two-seat general-purpose aircraft was for ten years ubiquitous east of Suez in several roles, including bombing and army cooperation on the NW Frontier of India. Eight RAF squadrons of Westland Wapitis were deployed across the Middle East and India for over a decade, well into World War II. During that time several squadrons detached their aircraft to Oman. The solar topees ('Bombay Bowlers') were often worn by pilots and air-gunners instead of flying helmets.

Today, the very latest and most modern aircraft in the inventory of the Oman Armed Forces is the Westland Super Lynx. Following a distinguished line of flying machines, the multi role, twin engined, Super Lynx is the most successful British helicopter and is used by Armed Forces and Navies all over the world. In contrast to the simple Wapiti, the Super Lynx comes equipped with the latest "glass" cockpit making it one of the most advanced helicopter cockpits available today. With improved performance and modern systems, the Super Lynx 300 provides a versatile capability covering anti-surface warfare, anti-submarine warfare, maritime patrol, search and rescue, casualty evacuation and utility transport. The Lynx holds the World Class E1e speed record for helicopters at an amazing 400.87 km/hr!

THE VERY FIRST FLYING MACHINE TO LAND IN Omani territorial waters was a Short Singapore of Number 203 Squadron based in Basrah, in Iraq. The squadron was formed on the 1st January 1929 when a Flight Lieutenant Revington arrived in Basrah. On the 10th January, he sailed in HMS Lopin to recce suitable alighting areas on the Trucial Coast, calling at Dubai, Sharjah and Ras Al Khaimah. He returned to Basra on 24th January 1929 when the very first three Singapore flying boats landed on the Shatt al Arab waterway. By April 1929, the flying boats were very frequent visitors around the Trucial States and made their first flight to Oman in May 1929. The flying boats made a big impact. The inset picture of a dhow shows, at the peak of her jack staff is a small model flying boat, a popular emblem throughout the Gulf. Each biplane flying boat carried a crew of five. Unlike the

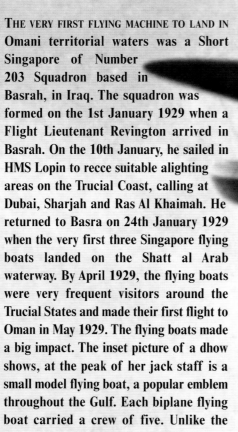

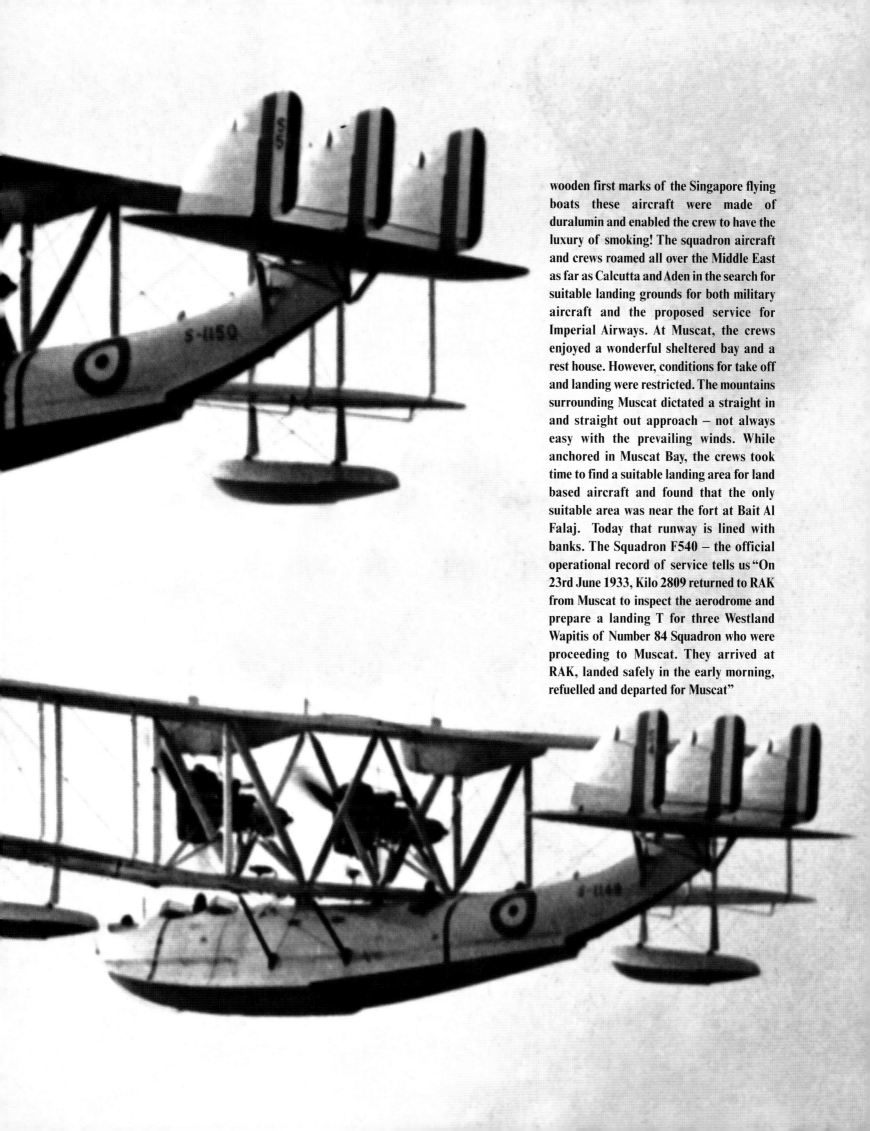

wooden first marks of the Singapore flying boats these aircraft were made of duralumin and enabled the crew to have the luxury of smoking! The squadron aircraft and crews roamed all over the Middle East as far as Calcutta and Aden in the search for suitable landing grounds for both military aircraft and the proposed service for Imperial Airways. At Muscat, the crews enjoyed a wonderful sheltered bay and a rest house. However, conditions for take off and landing were restricted. The mountains surrounding Muscat dictated a straight in and straight out approach – not always easy with the prevailing winds. While anchored in Muscat Bay, the crews took time to find a suitable landing area for land based aircraft and found that the only suitable area was near the fort at Bait Al Falaj. Today that runway is lined with banks. The Squadron F540 – the official operational record of service tells us "On 23rd June 1933, Kilo 2809 returned to RAK from Muscat to inspect the aerodrome and prepare a landing T for three Westland Wapitis of Number 84 Squadron who were proceeding to Muscat. They arrived at RAK, landed safely in the early morning, refuelled and departed for Muscat"

IN THE PERIOD FROM 1929 TO 1931, THE Singapore flying boats and Wapiti land planes made great efforts to find suitable routes and landing grounds for the aircraft of Imperial Airways. The original route had been flown across Persia (present day Iran) but political problems forced Imperial to route round the southern Gulf and the need to prove the new route became urgent. At that time, Gwadar (now in present day Pakistan) was part of the Oman Empire and permission had already been given for Imperial Airways to establish a staging post there. The archive tells us that the matter was becoming fractious. A letter to the Air Ministry from Imperial Airways, The Airway Terminus, Victoria Station (tel. Victoria 2211) says, "While I am glad to know that at Gwadar there is, at any rate, one place where we can land, I must say that it does not provide an altogether satisfactory solution to the problem. Having left Karachi, we shall, obviously, on occasions, encounter headwinds and we shall arrive at Gwadar somewhat behind schedule. The onward flight to Sharjah is more uncertain since Sharjah is on the eastern side of an important range of mountains, and we know that conditions can be entirely different on the two sides of this mountain range. Furthermore, if the mountain tops are covered in cloud, we will not be able to fly around them as it is beyond the petrol endurance of the "aircraft". The problem was over come by fitting extra fuel tanks to the Handley Page HP 42, at that time the largest civil aircraft in the world. It was a biplane with a wingspan of 130 feet with a flying range of 420 miles sufficient to cover the 420 miles form Sharjah to Gwadar in five and a half hours. Today, though Gwadar is no longer part of the Oman Empire, Oman Air still make regular flight to this location for many Omani, especially the Baluchis, still regard Gwadar as home. With the outbreak of the Second World War, the HP42 continued in service with the RAF while the Short Sunderland flying boasts patrolled the Indian Ocean and the Gulf of Oman in the hunt for U-boats.

THE SULTAN SAID BIN TAIMUR REQUESTED BRITISH HELP IN A STRUGGLE that became known as the Jebel Akhdar War (1957-59) – help in suppressing the tribal rebellion in the Interior by the turbulent followers of the Imam of Oman. British help was provided first by airpower then by seconded officers with limited units of ground troops and finally, the Special Air Service. Air attacks were flown from RAF Sharjah and RAF Masirah, on the forts and towers of towns at the foot of the Jebel Akhdar – Nizwa, Tanuf, Birket Al-Maws and Bahla – beginning on 24 July 1957. Later (in the second phase of the War) as two Omani/British columns converged on the area from north and south, RAF airpower assumed a softening-up role in support, bombing and strafing rebel positions near the towns. Later still, in the third phase, RAF air-attacks concentrated on the besieged Jebel Plateau on top of the mountains, on the disputed wadi track approaches and on the entrenched rebel positions on the rim of the Plateau and around the town of Saiq. Much was also made of 'firepower demonstrations', rocketing and bombing the huge upright limestone barrier slabs, which reared up for thousands of feet and made the Jebel Plateau so inaccessible. The rebels held out in the fastness of their Jebel strongholds apparently unmoved by imminent destruction from the skies. The air attacks continued in support until the end of the 'Jebel War' when, on 26 January 1959, the last rebel strongholds were finally stormed by the SAS and the rebellion died out. Thereafter, the RAF supported the troops on the plateau by flying from an airfield on the plain. The airfield on the plain was called Firq and the airfield on the plateau was called Saiq. After four hazardous supply runs over parts of the rebel held territory, the pilots were awarded a special tie. Meanwhile, the young Sultan Qaboos graduated from the Royal Military Academy of Sandhurst in England and then served with the Cameron Highlanders, a Regiment of the British army of the Rhine. Today's modern aircraft are refuelled and can take off in peace.

THE DISCOVERY OF OIL ON THE ARABIAN PENINSULA STIRRED THE troubled waters of revolt. The basic cause of the revolt was widespread tribal discontent, where tribal feud was a timeless part of life among the fiercely independent Jebali tribes. The revolt was against the rule of Sultan Said Bin Taimur in Dhofar and the prospecting oil companies. The Mecom Oil Company had begun prospecting inland from Salalah across the Jebel at a camp in the Nejd they called Midway. They had their own port at Raysut and various airstrips with names such as Idlewild, Orly and Pasadena where the support aircraft brought vital equipment. The first targets of the war were Mecom trucks along the Midway Road. However, the war took a more sinister turn when Russian and Chinese backed communist rebels were re-organized into the People's Front for the Liberation of Oman and the Arabian Gulf (PFLOAG). The target was now not just Oman but control of the Gulf and the vital Straights of Hormuz. Initially, the PFLOAG seized the initiative, denied the Mountains to the Sultan's forces and attempted to carry the war down from the Jebel on to the Plain posing a great threat to Sultan Said Bin Taimur himself who lived in Salalah. It was at this point in the war when Sultan Qaboos assumed power.

WHEN HIS MAJESTY SULTAN QABOOS ASSUMED POWER in 1970, the fortunes of war reversed. Support for the new Sultan came not only from Britain but also from Abu Dhabi, Saudi Arabia, an entire brigade of troops from Iran, complete with support aircraft and helicopters and perhaps the most remarkable gift of all – a complete air force in the shape of 32 Hawker Hunters. This "gift" was from King Hussein of Jordan and the aircraft arrived in March 1975. The war was turned with the powerful Hunters in the air supporting Alvis Saladin armoured cars on the ground, and was declared over by Royal decree on the 12th December 1975.

THE MODERN AIRCRAFT OF TODAY ARE supplied by Boeing who equips the Royal Flight, shown here during a State departure and a fleet of Oman Air. Oman serves an international spread of destinations including Bombay, Trivandram and Dhaka, and supports all the operations of the Petroleum Development Operation throughout Oman. The Royal Air Force of Oman still retains the Hunters from Jordan and also the Jaguar aircraft, which perform ultra low level flying and Royal escort duties.

Chapter 4
The Discovery of Oil

NEARLY 70 YEARS AGO A GROUP OF PIONEERING GEOLOGISTS TREKKED across the deserts of Oman in search of the elusive "black gold". It was a hot, dirty task and required tough men to endure the extremes of the desert - where temperatures reached up to 55 degrees Celsius and much of the work was carried out on foot. But the world economy demanded oil to fuel its growth and, hard work or not, it had to be found. Nowhere was the hunt more intense than the Middle East but the first exploration of Oman, by D'Arcy Exploration Company, failed to turn up any trace of the valuable energy source and the search was soon abandoned. Although

efforts were resumed shortly after World War II, it wasn't until 1962 that the first commercial find was made, at Yibal in northern Oman. The following year geologists discovered the Natih field near Fuhud and Oman's oil industry was born. A 279-kilometre pipeline was built from Fuhud to the coast at Mina Al-Fahal and the first oil was exported in 1967.

Towards the end of 1959, a Royal Charter had granted BP the right to market oil products in Oman. The charter has been extended several times and has seen years of unprecedented progress, both for BP in Oman and for the country as a whole. BP's operations

cover a multi-million dollar tank farm and depot at Mina al Fahal, the expansive oil complex near Muscat and the nerve centre of the Sultanate's massive oil programme. As the result of oil income, life in Oman has changed radically. In the space of one generation, Oman has emerged from a virtually medieval slumber into the mainstream of the twentieth century - a phenomenal achievement. On his accession, H. H. Sultan Qaboos immediately embarked on a process of modernisation - a dynamic development that continues to this day. Oman had a very long way to go. Just ten kilometres of tarmac road served the nation in 1970. The number of hospitals in

a land the size of Great Britain could be counted on the fingers of one hand. There was just one school. With revenue coming in from rapidly increasing oil exports, Sultan Qaboos and his government set about addressing the considerable problems of this newly prosperous nation tucked on the southernmost corner of the Arabian Peninsula. Evidence of the success of Oman's development programme is not difficult to find in the 1990s. The Sultanate today boasts hundreds of schools, hospitals and clinics - part of a burgeoning infrastructure supported by many thousands of kilometres of tarmac road.

OMAN NOW PRODUCES AROUND **900,000** barrels
of oil a day with **70** fields spanning more than
1200 kilometres from Al Dahira in the north
to Dhahabun in the south.   Thousands of
people are employed in exploration,
production and development. Countless more
work in related industries. Getting to the oil
has not been easy. Oman's complex geology
and often-hostile terrain make recovering
petroleum reserves here more expensive and
more difficult than for most other Gulf
States. The majority of its fields are also
smaller, with wells averaging just **600** barrels
a day compared with up to **10** times that much
from neighbouring oil-producing countries,
so new technology has to be applied to make
drilling more economical. The search for oil
is never ending as the country tries to
maintain production while adding to its
reserves, which stand at around **5** billion
barrels, or about **0.5** per cent of the world's
proven oil reserves. At the current rate of
production Oman has about **17** years of oil
reserves remaining, although further
discoveries, improved technology and
curbing of production should enable it to
prolong the industry's life here.

IN 1972, THE ORIGINAL BP OPERATION WAS tiny, largely concerned with the supply of aviation fuel to the Sultan's Armed Forces and to the country's only international airport at Bait Al Falaj. The first BP manager wrote, "The BP office at Riyam Bay wasn't much more than a shed next to the powerhouse. Craggy mountains surround the bay and whenever it rained, which can be quite often in Oman, one couldn't possibly work in the office for at least two days because it was flooded, washed out, even after just a slight shower. Up until 1972, a company dhow laden with 45-gallon drums would be unloaded at the port by a far-from-hi-tech disgorging operation involving floating each and every barrel to the beach and rolling them ashore. The product would then be taken by Bedford truck to the company's fuelling facilities at Bait Al Falaj. Between 1972 and 1975, when BP transferred its operations from Riyam Bay to Mina al Fahal, drums of jet A-1 and Avgas imports came by road from Dubai in the United Arab Emirates. Automotive products arrived by coastal tanker and were discharged via a submarine pipeline". Today things are very different. No longer does the country depend on the importation of refined products. Gasoline, kerosene, jet fuel and diesel have all been refined at the government refinery since 1982. From these early days BP's business in Oman has expanded with the economy. The company currently handles over 250,000 tonnes a year of automotive products as well as 2,500 tonnes of lubricants, most of which are blended at the Melubco plant (in which BP Middle East holds a 49% stake) in the United Arab Emirates. BP supplies and maintains over sixty dealer-operated filling stations throughout the Sultanate, in a retail operation that stretches the length and breadth of the land.

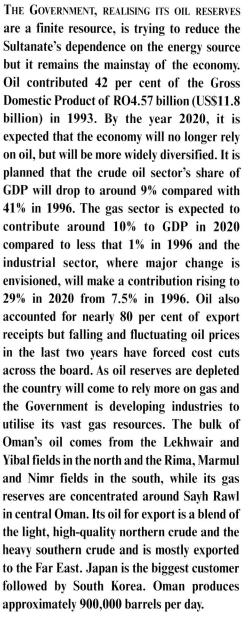

THE GOVERNMENT, REALISING ITS OIL RESERVES are a finite resource, is trying to reduce the Sultanate's dependence on the energy source but it remains the mainstay of the economy. Oil contributed 42 per cent of the Gross Domestic Product of RO4.57 billion (US$11.8 billion) in 1993. By the year 2020, it is expected that the economy will no longer rely on oil, but will be more widely diversified. It is planned that the crude oil sector's share of GDP will drop to around 9% compared with 41% in 1996. The gas sector is expected to contribute around 10% to GDP in 2020 compared to less that 1% in 1996 and the industrial sector, where major change is envisioned, will make a contribution rising to 29% in 2020 from 7.5% in 1996. Oil also accounted for nearly 80 per cent of export receipts but falling and fluctuating oil prices in the last two years have forced cost cuts across the board. As oil reserves are depleted the country will come to rely more on gas and the Government is developing industries to utilise its vast gas resources. The bulk of Oman's oil comes from the Lekhwair and Yibal fields in the north and the Rima, Marmul and Nimr fields in the south, while its gas reserves are concentrated around Sayh Rawl in central Oman. Its oil for export is a blend of the light, high-quality northern crude and the heavy southern crude and is mostly exported to the Far East. Japan is the biggest customer followed by South Korea. Oman produces approximately 900,000 barrels per day.

THE RACE TO DEVELOP A GAS EXPORT INDUSTRY IN OMAN IS NOW gathering speed with the US$ 6 billion Liquefied Natural Gas (LNG) project now on stream. The LNG employed more than 7000 workers at the height of construction and is boosting Oman's economy by reducing its dependence on oil. Construction commenced in 1996 and the first exports were made in April 2000. The project is divided into two parts upstream and downstream. It involves collecting gas from three main fields in central Oman and

piping it 350 kilometres to the coast at Al Ghalilah, near Sur, where it is liquefied before being loaded onto insulated tankers and shipped to customers. Petroleum Development Oman (PDO) on behalf of the Government manages upstream operations, while Oman LNG, a joint venture company with seven shareholders, including the Government, manages the downstream phase. A total of 7 trillion cubic feet of gas has been committed to the project from Oman's current estimated reserves of 20 trillion

cubic feet, which will enable the plant to run for 20 years. The LNG project is being developed separately from an ambitious plan to build a 1500 kilometre underwater pipeline to the Indian state of Maharashtra. The US$2.8 billion pipeline will reach depths of 3.5 kilometres - five times deeper than any submarine pipeline ever built.

THE GENERAL TELECOMMUNICATIONS Organisation (GTO) was established in 1980 as a government owned entity. Sixteen years later, in 1996, bold privatisation plans were announced and the Royal Decree, number 46/99, issued on 19th July 1999, converted GTO into an Omani closed stock holding company know as OMANTEL. In 1970, there were only 557 working analogue lines covering Muscat and Muttrah, while international calls were made using HF radio. In 1998, all telephone lines became digital and now there are more than half a million lines. International calls can be made to anywhere in the world using the latest satellite equipment. The monochrome photograph was taken in Salalah in the 1970s where a passing camel is scratching his back, not putting up telephone poles.

Chapter 5
Muscat – The Capital

"MUSCAT BAY IS, TO MY MIND, THE MOST wonderful that nature and art could ever devise. It is surrounded in deep semicircle by high precipitous rocks, which the Portuguese have topped with watchtowers, each equipped in the same way and painted with white lime. We could only marvel at how guns could have been carried up such steep inclines".

Engelbert Kaempfer 1688

"*Since Muscat is entirely surrounded by mountains, it can be approached by land only on donkey-back. A watchtower is placed at the narrowest point between the rocks, about half a mile or a third of a mile from the town gate. At about a similar distance beyond the first hill, drinking water channels are led to the town, where two cisterns convey it to ships and other receptacles. For the clear, sweet water of Muscat you pay one rupee for about 290 litres. Though we ordered the water early in the morning, it was not supplied until midday because, they said, both cistern had been completely empty, so they had to await fresh supplies from the hills*".

Engelbert Kaempfer 1688

"*THE HOUSES ARE SOMEWHAT SARACENIC IN general style. They all have two floors, and some even three. The walls of the upper rooms are divided into innumerable openings by long, narrow windows, so that air may come freely in from all quarters. No one lives on the ground floors, which are used as lumber or storerooms. The roofs form the bedchambers; no one can sleep indoors during the hot weather on account of the stifling heat. When the shumal, or hot wind from the desert, blows, the sleepers are during the night watered, like plants, with a watering pot. This practice may account for the fact that muscular rheumatism is by no means unknown in Muscat*".

Gratton Geary, Editor of the Times of India, March 1878

IN 1940, ALAN VILLIERS VISITED MUSCAT. *"Muscat looked picturesque as one came over the pass and there were good buildings: the Sultans' Palace, the British residency and the houses of loading merchants. Across the bay was a large Portuguese fort. The guns in the fort were a mixed battery of ancient muzzle loaders which included iron guns from India and Yorkshire and two beautifully carved old Portuguese guns"*.

Today, Jalali Fort has been restored and a new magnificent Palace welcomes Heads of State from around the world.

"*ACROSS THE PLAIN TO RUI [SIC], A SMALL hamlet, inhabited by tillers of the soil. Here is plenty of good water in wells, which are about fifty feet deep.*
At least half a dozen water drawing machines are creaking away. Here are grown nearly all the vegetables, which come to Muscat – onions, lettuce, radishes, brinjals, sugar cane, maize etc. There are some fine mango and tamarind trees, and many dates; in fact, the valley for half a mile is a regular garden".

Captain Arthur W Stiffe, 1897

THE PORTUGUESE BUILT THE TOWERING structure of Fort Mirani shortly after they captured Muscat in 1507 AD. With Fort Mirani and the sister fort of Jalali, the Portuguese controlled all the trade routes from the Far East to Europe. Below the fort, a mosque has existed since Islam first reached Muscat. The simple houses below the fort belonged to the fishermen who to this day have special permission from the Sultan to have the use of Muscat harbour.

Chapter 6
Salalah – The Garden City of Dhofar

"THE QARA MOUNTAINS ... WHAT A GLORIOUS place! Mountains three thousand feet high basking above a tropical ocean, the seaward slopes velvety with waving jungle, their roofs fragrant with rolling yellow meadows, beyond which the mountains slope northwards to a red sandstone steppe".

Bertram Thomas, 1928

Salalah, which lies within the Dhofar region of southern Oman, is a unique location, geographically and historically. The town sits at the center of a sweeping crescent of silvery white sand stretching 60 km from the rocky headlands of Raysut Harbour to the tomb of Bin Ali at Mirbat.

Behind the beach, lies a crescent shaped plain. In turn, the plain is surrounded by low but imposing jebels (hills), which are covered with trees and vegetation of an almost impossible green colour. This green colour is the result of yet another aspect of the uniqueness of Salalah. Every year, on 17th June, the Southwest monsoon winds, (which pushed Omani sailors home from Zanzibar), bring moisture laden air to Dhofar which ascends up and over the Qara Mountains forming layers of monsoon cloud and attendant drizzle.

Dawn was the time for the caravan trails to depart and when the sun reached high in the sky, they rested their camels until afternoon prayers. When the sun had gone down and the heat reduced, they continued their journey until darkness. Fishermen and divers left early in the morning in summer and returned by noon, going out again after afternoon prayers. Fish were left on the shore to dry in the sun. Farmers used the sun to dry lemons, dates and other agricultural produce. In the past, people believed the heat of the sun cured skin diseases and rheumatism.

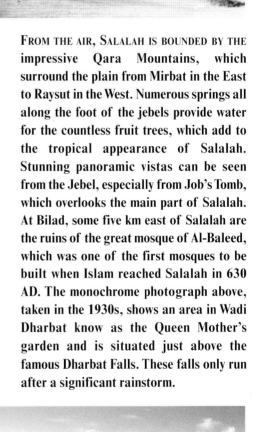

FROM THE AIR, SALALAH IS BOUNDED BY THE impressive Qara Mountains, which surround the plain from Mirbat in the East to Raysut in the West. Numerous springs all along the foot of the jebels provide water for the countless fruit trees, which add to the tropical appearance of Salalah. Stunning panoramic vistas can be seen from the Jebel, especially from Job's Tomb, which overlooks the main part of Salalah. At Bilad, some five km east of Salalah are the ruins of the great mosque of Al-Baleed, which was one of the first mosques to be built when Islam reached Salalah in 630 AD. The monochrome photograph above, taken in the 1930s, shows an area in Wadi Dharbat know as the Queen Mother's garden and is situated just above the famous Dharbat Falls. These falls only run after a significant rainstorm.

THE TRANSHIPMENT TRAFFIC OF THE MIDDLE EAST IS CONCENTRATED IN A SMALL NUMBER OF HUB PORTS, many of them almost exclusively devoted to this activity. In 1990, three ports accounted for almost all of the region's transhipment, namely Dubai in the Arabian Gulf, on the west coast of the United Arab Emirates, Fujeirah on the east coast of the United Arab Emirates on the Indian Ocean and Colombo in Sri Lanka. By 2000 Colombo and Dubai were still the leading ports but Fujairah had lessened in importance and was overtaken by both Khor Fakkan, adjacent to Fujeirah, and Salalah in southern Oman. Between them these five ports account for almost 90% of the region's transhipment activity. Salalah's impact has been most marked on the ports of Dubai and Colombo. 1999 was Salalah's first full year of operations when the market share implications became very clear. Dubai lost approximately 7% market share whilst Colombo lost around 4%. During 2000, Dubai and Colombo lost a further market share to Salalah, albeit not as much as the previous year. The only other port to gain a market share in 2000 was Aden on the southern coast of Yemen. By the year 2000, Salalah's share of the transhipment market had reached 17.4%. And growing.

THE AERIAL VIEW OF SALALAH AND AL HISN Palace was probably taken in 1971. There is no tarmac road, the main road to the west is being watered and the wet tracks of the truck can be seen forming a circle in the yard of the old hospital. The road grading to the top of the picture is the new road leading to the Royal Air Force base. In the middle of the crossroads is the wooden box with shade where a policeman stood to direct the traffic. At this time, there was open access to the square and the area of the souq to the east of the palace. The haphazard layout of supplies on the beach suggests that it was landed on the beach from shashah stitched boats transporting the goods from dhows offshore, rather than having arrived by truck from the new port of Raysut. Today the layout of the palace grounds has changed substantially. The old mosque has been renovated and now stands in a landscaped garden inside the gates.

WITH THE ENDING OF THE DHOFAR WAR, IT became customary to invite the Jebali hill tribesmen to descend to the plain and celebrate National Day. Here, the combined tribes of Jabalis circle and dance around the main square of Al Hisn Palace. The Jebali language is a spoken language only – there is no written form and it appears inevitable that the language will disappear now that all the children in Dhofar are educated in Arabic. His Majesty has made several appointments and commissions to collect anthropological data of the Jebali tribes and their language and also of the flora and fauna of their hilltop habitat.

THERE ARE ALREADY a number of Free Zones in existence in the Middle East region and in general terms, there are certain basic factors necessary that any Free Zone must possess in order to succeed. These apply regardless of the worldwide location. In order to be successful; a Free Zone needs to offer more than just fiscal incentives or benefits to its users. Ideally, a Free Zone needs to be located in, or very close to, a successful commercial port or trading centre that benefits from a high frequency and a full range of different shipping lines calling. A politically stable and economically strong country is also very important to the potential success of the Free Zone. Salalah Port Services (SPS) obtained approval from the Omani government to establish the Salalah Free Zone Port Company (SPFZ) during 2000. The decision to develop the Free Zone was based on a desire to increase both export and local traffic for the port itself. At the same time, the Omani government had been under pressure to promote non-oil sector initiatives after 24 months of volatile oil prices. SPFZ is a joint venture with SPS taking a 20% stake, the Omani government 40% and Hillwood, a Dallas (Texas)-based developer, also taking 40%. Hillwood has also signed an agreement to manage the zone. Hillwood was established in 1987 by Ross Perot Jr and has subsequently developed 25,000 acres in 25 cities, predominantly in the US. The company has foreign trade zone experience at the 9,600-acre industrial airport it developed in Dallas. SPFZ is to be developed in phases as part of an overall master plan that will cater for a wide range of different activities. These cover distribution, industrial, light manufacturing, container freight station, "high-tech" service, office and retail uses. Electronics and IT-related industries in particular are being targeted. Government officials are also hopeful that SPFZ will mean a significant number of new jobs, especially for the local population

Chapter 7
Sports, Leisure & Tourism

THE MONOCHROME PHOTOGRAPH SHOWS THE OLD TRACK TO SIDAB and the village Quantab beyond. The Al Bhustan Palace Hotel was built in 1984 and was voted as the best hotel in the world shortly after it opened. Today, expansive efforts are being made to develop the tourism industry of Oman in an effort to employ large numbers of the growing population. Oman has one of the most beautiful coastlines in the world summed up

by H.E. Maqbool bin Ali Sultan, The Minister of Commerce & Industry who said "*Oman's rich cultural, historical and geological backdrop, its pristine beaches washed by the waters of the Gulf of Oman, the Arabian Sea and the Arabian Gulf, certainly offer an unparalled canvas of potential*".

The inset picture shows HSBC's hot air balloon being flown during the National Day Celebrations.

OMAN IS A PARADISE FOR ADVENTURE TRAVEL AND specialized tours are becoming most popular. Heide Beal Tours offer guided expeditions to some of the hidden but spectacular parts of Jebel Akhdar. The main picture shows the waterfalls in Wadi Daiqa but perhaps the most adventurous tour is the descent of Wadi Bani Auf. Above Bilad Sayt, the wadi narrows into a cleft only eight feet wide. The descent that follows involves a series of waterfalls where the traveller has to jump into the pool below. The first big jump is the point of no return since there is no way of climbing back up. Depending on the amount of recent rain, some of the falls are dry but with deep pools below. Travellers are advised to be good swimmers and reasonably fit and can be assured that they will get totally wet. The descent should never be attempted if rain is at all likely since the gorge becomes a raging torrent.

OMAN'S SEAS AND COASTS HAVE BOUNTIFUL RESOURCES THAT contribute to the economic, social and cultural well being of the country. The beauty of the coast attracts new housing development and recreation. The fertile coastal plains and underground water support agriculture and the flat coastal lands are suited to industry. The waters themselves maintain fisheries, while the deep sheltered bays lure enthusiasts of marine sports. Numerous archaeological sites hold secrets of life and environment in Oman in ancient times.

In 1984, as a further response to the development, the Ministry of Commerce and Industry contracted the International Union for Conservation of Nature and Natural Resources (IUCN) to prepare Coastal Zone Management Plans for sections of the coast. The results showed that the Damaniyats islands alone have at least two-and-a-half times more hawksbill turtles nesting there than had previously been estimated for the whole of Oman.

The hawksbill turtle is one of the world's more endangered species, which has been widely slaughtered elsewhere for its thick plates of "tortoise shell." A number of factors make this a difficult species to manage. It nests in low numbers scattered over a vast area. Also, it is a small species which buries its eggs in much more shallow holes than the larger species turtle. For this reason, foxes are able to locate and unearth the eggs with considerable success, and as many as 50-70% of all clutches layed on mainland beaches are lost in this way. Thus the Damaniyats islands with their large numbers of hawksbill turtles nesting in a confined and easily managed area, which is free of mainland predators, provide an unusual management opportunity, and are of global importance for the conservation of this endangered species. Although tourists cannot land on the islands without a special permit, scuba diving is encouraged in these pristine waters.

WHEN THE REVEREND ZWEMER FIRST reached the mountains, he observed;

"*The most populous and fertile district of the highlands of Oman is Jebel Akhdar, which is also the best known. The fertility of this region is wonderful and is striking contrast with the barren rocks of so large a part of the coast. With a semi-tropical climate, an elevation of 3,000 to 5,000 feet, and abundant springs, the wadys and*

oases of Oman have awakened the delight and amazement of every traveller who has ventured to explore them. Water, the one priceless treasure in all Arabia, here issues in perennial streams from many rocky clefts and is most carefully husbanded by the ingenuity of the people for wide irrigation by means of canals or watercourses called falaj".

Reverend S.M. Zwemer, 1911.

Today, a group of adventurers swim up Wadi Shab located half way between Muscat and Sur. On the coast is a shallow lagoon which one has to wade across before walking through pleasing palm gardens. After about a one-hour walk, the wadi narrows when travellers are obliged to swim to proceed further. The highest point of Jebel Akhdar (the green mountain) is Jebel Shams (the mountain of the sun), which at 3,009 metres above sea level, is the highest mountain in Oman. Not far from Shams is the sprawling up land plateau of Saiq, which is ideal for hiking even in the middle of summer. At the edge of the plateau, overlooking the steep wadis to the valley floor, are a number of terraced villages where roses, grapes and the best garlic in the world, grow. Garlic from Jebel Akhdar has been sought after for centuries dating back to its use by the Babylonians and Egyptians who sealed it in their tombs. Greek athletes at the original Olympiad in 776 BC chewed garlic for stamina and the father of medicine, Hippocrates, recommended its curative properties.

THE MUSANDAM PENINSULA IS ONE OF THE MOST DRAMATIC landscapes in the world. Towering peaks, deep clear water in fjord like wadis and a wild natural beauty unlike any other place on the Arabian Peninsula. The best way to explore the Musandam is by sea and from Khasab it is possible to hire a dhow and tour the inlets. Within Khor As Sham is Telegraph Island with the remains of the telegraph station built in 1864. The schooner "Charlotte Anne" now offers a new service for tourist. The schooner can carry a party of 14 passengers in seagoing comfort to explore the Musandam at their leisure. Dolphins abound and there is good chance of seeing whales and whale sharks. In the various khors are magnificent dive sites with crystal clear water, submarine caves and an untouched variety of fish life.

Wadi Daiqa, in northern Oman, is also known as "The Devil's Gap" a feature that can easily be seen from the ocean by passing sailors. The experience of modern adventurers is just as poignant as the first explorers. In 1884 Lt. Col Samuel Miles first travelled through Wadi Daiqa and wrote:

"We found ourselves at the entrance of a great cleft, which is as sharp and abrupt as if we were entering the portals of some monstrous castle and stood immured within its massive walls. Towering loftily, sheer and perpendicular above the narrow floor, the huge walls of rock give the appearance as if the mountain range had suddenly been split in twain from the base to the summit by some convulsion of nature, exhibiting a singular illustration of impressive grandeur"

"After heavy rain, the volume of water flowing through this chasm must be enormous, and the surging and raging torrent must be a magnificent sight. It not infrequently happens that travellers and caravans coming from Kuryat [sic] are engulfed and overwhelmed by the sudden rise and rush of the stream, as the innumerable tributaries and affluents in a drainage area of some 200 square miles, swelling after rain, would concentrate at the gorge with marvellous rapidity and force, and form a mighty and irresistible wave, destroying everything in its path. The peculiar character of this chasm, and the grand and picturesque scenery of its surroundings, create an impression on the mind which is not easily effaced."

Lieutenant-Colonel Samuel Miles, February 1884

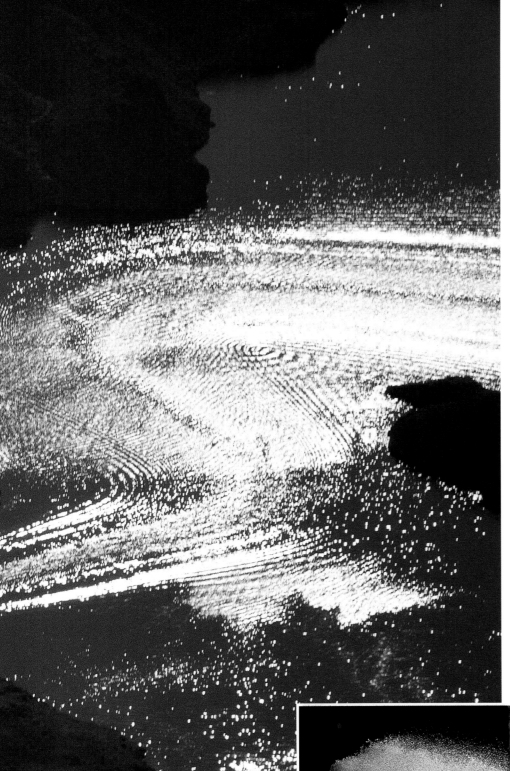

EVEN BEFORE COMING TO OMAN A QUICK, cursory glance at a World Atlas shows the country to have a long coastline. The coupling of the temperatures of the Tropic of Cancer tapped by the Arabian Sea offer an ideal recipe for any water sports enthusiast. From swimming and sailing to water skiing and windsurfing, every opportunity exists for water sport enthusiast in Oman. Bandar Khayran, about 20-25 minutes from Muscat is totally sheltered from the sea with a network of winding channels, deserted islands and large open beaches. This bay is a stunning work of nature, hidden in the far corner is a fishing village with the dirt road from Tiwi snaking behind it. The conditions here are ideal for the novice and expert alike with plenty of sheltered calm water and space for everyone. For those who have never tried skiing the bay presents perfect conditions - almost mirror surfaces, warm water and imposing surroundings. The pure exhilaration of skiing across the water at 40 kph offers a challenge that few can refuse.

Chapter 8
Natural History & Culture

LIKE FATHER, LIKE SON. FOR THOUSANDS OF YEARS, SONS HAVE HELPED their fathers to bring home the catch. The seas that surround Oman teem with an abundance of fish. The relative remoteness of sections of this coast has helped to preserve the natural beauty of the landscape and the wildlife habitats. Here, in Salalah, the vast sweep of the crescent shaped beach is interspersed by rocky headlands and cliffs that jut into the sea and provide ideal vantage points for observing life below. Although the value of coastal scenery is intangible and difficult to quantify, it has social and cultural significance for Omanis and tourists alike and this area offers dramatic scenery, greater contact with nature, and opportunities for wilderness recreation.

THE ARABIAN LEOPARD (PANTHERA PARDUS NIMR), OR NIMR IN ARABIC, is the largest surviving member of the cat family in the Arabian Peninsula and once inhabited the mountainous regions of Jordan, Oman, Saudi Arabia, United Arab Emirates and Yemen. Persecuted by man, the Arabian leopard is today on the Critically Endangered list (IUCN Red List) and the subject of international conservation efforts. In Saudi Arabia and Yemen there are believed to be small isolated numbers, while perhaps just five animals survive in the eastern region of the United Arab Emirates adjacent to Oman. In Oman the leopard, qeydhar in Jebali, can still be found in Jebel Samhan Nature Reserve and elsewhere in the mountains of Dhofar Governorate. To help support the wild populations Oman established the first captive-breeding programme for the Arabian leopard in 1985. Leopards from this programme helped establish a similar programme in the Emirate of Sharjah. Scientists working in the mountains of Dhofar have used camera-traps to collect the first ecological data on the Arabian leopard and in 2001 satellite GPS collars were fitted to a leopard in order to study their movements in the wild. This information is essential to the understanding of the requirements of the leopard and for ensuring that it has a secure future in the wild. This remarkable photograph was taken using an automatic camera triggered by the Leopard crossing an infrared beam. The crews of the Royal Flight had placed the camera in the high jebels. When the leopard cut the beam in mid stride, the camera emits a "click" just before the shutter opens causing the Leopard to "look" at the camera. The inset picture shows an oil painting by the world famous artist, David Shepherd OBE. David is famous throughout the world for his paintings of endangered wild life. The proceeds of his paintings fund the 'David Shepherd Wild Life Foundation'.

HEAD ADORNMENTS ARE POPULAR IN OMAN, and moon or star symbols often appear on them. The '*qam*', which goes under the chin, is attached to the headscarf by means of ornate triangular hooks that feature the moon and stars symbols. Unmarried girls and even babies generally wear the '*harf*', which hangs down the centre of the forehead. Traditional Omani jewellery design is quite ornate and often features Qur'anic script, geometric, floral or celestial decorations showing the sun, moon and stars. There is an Omani bracelet or anklet that is called a '*kamar*', which means moon. It is in the shape of a crescent moon and often features elaborate decoration. The '*hirz*' necklace is a traditional Omani necklace, made to hold a small copy of The Holy Qur'an or specially selected verses. It is made of finely crafted silver that is often incised some necklaces have chains hanging from them with bells and crescent-moon pendants (*al hirz al masalsal*). Another necklace, known as the '*qursh mkahhal*', features a star or flower symbol as the focal point of a large disc pendant. The many elaborate designs originated in ancient times when Omani sailors forged their way to India and China, and local merchants established a trading empire in East Africa. The prosperous trading enabled Omani goldsmiths and silversmiths to develop their techniques with influences from many different countries.

THE WHALE SHARK CAN BE EASILY SEEN OFF THE OMAN COAST FROM Musandam, Muscat to Dhofar. This huge harmless fish often swims close to the shore or below the sea cliff around Lima Rock and near Khor Rori. It was here that a certain fighter pilot took a piggyback ride by clutching onto the fin of the shark. The shark accelerated, the pilot lost his mask and was obliged to let go. On the shoreline of Ras Al Hadd and Ras Al Junayz, at the most easterly point of the Arabian Peninsula, is the place to see Green Turtles. Oman has the largest population of Green Turtles in the world and they now are within a

protected area. Sensitive supervision of the nature reserve encourages visitors not to disturb the turtles at night when they come up the beach to lay their eggs. Visitors are encourages to rise early with the dawn to see the turtles returning to the sea. Turtles mate in the sea and lay about three clutches of eggs in a season. The turtle digs a hole above the high water mark and lays about 100 eggs in the sand. The eggs hatch, almost simultaneously, after 55 days, the young hatchlings find their way to the surface of the sand and begin their perilous journey to the sea.

THOUSANDS OF YEARS AGO, SOHAR WAS THE FOCAL POINT OF returning seafarers for one simple reason; just inland from Sohar is a prominent white coloured mountain, which could be seen for many miles by inbound sailors. Sohar is reputed to be the home of' Sindbad The Sailor', the most famous of the Omani navigators. Today the white fort of Sohar is a well-presented museum. The museum's Askari guards war the traditional '*khanjar*' an unchanging symbol of Omani manhood. Outside the fort, Sohar is a changing place. Here are new industrial estates, mining towns, new ports and new fast road links to Muscat, some 220 km to the southeast and the UAE and Dubai, 180 km to the northwest.   Under the shade of a tree, the timeless practice of learning the Koran continues.

THE LEGEND OF THE UNICORN HAD ITS ORIGINS IN ARABIA. ARISTOTLE recorded that the people of Arabia bound the horns of young Oryx so that the horns grew as one. No one knows why or when such a practice originated but it was almost certain that this was the origin of the myth of the Unicorn. The Arabian Oryx belongs to the antelope family and lives, in central Oman, in one of the most harsh and dry climates on the Jiddat Al Harasis. There is almost no surface water on the plain and Oryx rely on moisture obtained from the leaves of trees during the very early morning when fog rolls

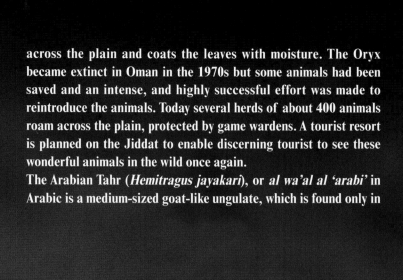

across the plain and coats the leaves with moisture. The Oryx became extinct in Oman in the 1970s but some animals had been saved and an intense, and highly successful effort was made to reintroduce the animals. Today several herds of about 400 animals roam across the plain, protected by game wardens. A tourist resort is planned on the Jiddat to enable discerning tourist to see these wonderful animals in the wild once again.

The Arabian Tahr (*Hemitragus jayakari*), or *al wa'al al 'arabi'* in Arabic is a medium-sized goat-like ungulate, which is found only in

the northern mountains of Oman, and in the United Arab Emirates close to the Oman border. It is described as Critically Endangered in the IUCN Red List and a high priority for regional conservation efforts. In 1975 a special wildlife guard force was established to protect the Tahr in the Wadi Sareen area of Oman. Scientific study of the Tahr started in 1975 in Wadi Sareen and in 1982 the first-ever captive breeding group was established. The formation of a new countrywide, wildlife guard force in the early 1990s helped provide further protection to the tahr. Today there is three main populations of Tahr in Oman (including Wadi Sareen Reserve) and other smaller populations are spread across the country.

WHILE RECORDS ARE SOMEWHAT VAGUE, IT IS probable that horses are not indigenous to Oman. Historical records indicate that in 500 BC, a stranger from what is now known as Saudi Arabia, one Malib bin Fahm, visited Nizwa riding a piebald charger. It can be reasonably assumed that when Malib bin Fahm and his companions left Oman they left behind, either by design or by accident, some of their horses. It can also be supposed that the ancestors of the present day Omani horsemen soon learned to master the horses that bin Mahib left behind and were able to breed from them. The next probable date of the arrival of horses in Oman is in the year 300 BC, when the country was visited by one of Alexander the Great's Admirals, Hieron of Soli. At that time he was resident in Persia. He landed in Musandam, and it can be assumed that he probably used horses to tour and explore the country. Naturally he would not have travelled alone and therefore we can presume that his escort of troops would also be mounted. In 630 AD Oman embraced the Islamic faith. Equestrianism is inherent in the preaching of the Prophet Mohammed (PBUH), who urged every male member of the faith not only to own a horse, but also that he should teach his sons how to ride.

The formation, by His Majesty Sultan Qaboos bin Said, of the Oman Equestrian Federation in November of 1985, only goes to strengthen the feeling that the day is not too far off when we will see an Omani competing at international level in one or all of the equestrian disciplines: show jumping, dressage, eventing, tent pegging (in itself still a cavalry activity) and carriage driving. Under the guidance of the Federation's President, His Highness Sayyid Shabib bin Taimur Al Said, all of these disciplines will be pursued. In the past twelve months both Bahrain and Kuwait have been declared free from African Horse Sickness - good news that brings the possibility of developing international champions from the Gulf that much closer.

Chapter 10
Authors
Acknowledgments

Ten years after the publication of my very first book, it was suggested by His Excellency Abdul Aziz Moh'd Al Rawas, then The Minister of Information of Oman for 30 years, that I should publish a sequel to my original book on Oman. My first book, "A Day Above Oman", which has now been reprinted eight times with only one revision, is a pictorial presentation of the beautiful environment of Oman and, as such, is timeless. This new book is entirely different in that it is acutely concerned with the passage of time and how specific locations have changed so dramatically over the past fifty years.

Ever since I commenced research on my book, "Now & Then – The Emirates", I have been storing information on the old archival

photographs of Oman, wherever I have found them. I received tremendous support from many officials in Oman. I would first like to thank His Excellency Sayyid Saif Bin Hamed Bin Hamoud Al Busaidi, The Minister of the Royal Diwan; His Excellency Mohammed Zubair, who granted me access to his wonderful museum and archive and kindly wrote the foreword; His Excellency Hamad Bin Moh'd Bin Mohsin Al Rashdy, The Minister of Information and His Excellency Salim Abdullah Al Ghazali, former Minister of Communication. Their staffs were most helpful and I would especially like to thank Salim M. Almahruqi, Dr Hamed Shadha Al Marjan and Amin Bin Yahya Al Riyami of the Ministry of Information and Mohammed Al Kamali and Sonia Teeneja of Al

Omeneya; Moh'd Mustafa, Royal Photographer for providing one my favourite pictures of all time, that of Sultan Qaboos greeting Her Majesty Queen Elizabeth II with The Duke Of Edinburgh shown on page 28/29 and also for the picture he took of myself meeting Sultan Qaboos shown on the rear flap; Ralph and Elizabeth Daly and especially Dr Andrew Spalton of the office of the Advisor for the Conservation of the Environment for the wonderful photograph of the leopard shown on page 110/111 and the Arabian Tahs on page 119 insert; Frank Haversedge and Antony Hayes; all of the Diwan of Royal Court.

When General Sir Peter De La Billiere launched his book"Looking For Trouble" (ISBN 1 873544-86-3) I had the pleasant experience

of flying him and a willing co-pilot, Ian Fairservice, in a brand new Commander 114B (courtesy of Sheikh Mishal Al Sabah) on a 4 day flight around the Gulf from Dubai to Kuwait then on to Bahrain and finally to Qatar. While the co pilot mastered the art of straight and level flying, the general gave me a first person account of his exploits, especially the final assault of Jebel Akhdar and the Mirbat incident. After four days of flight training, the co pilot completed a take off from Doha, flew reasonably straight and level to Dubai where he executed a passable landing. For those who seek deeper information about the Dhofar War, I can also recommend John Akehurst's book "We Won A War – The Campaign in Oman 1965 – 1975" ISBN 0-85955-091-5. Both books are a "good"read

I met many archivists once again and all were unfailingly helpful and though I was not able to use all the pictures that I found, I would like to thank all following archivists: Sarah White of the Zubair Museum archive for the tremendous support I received (page 10, 40 inset, 42, 56, 82/83, 83 inset, 88, 90/91 and 116); Jack Helton and Kutaiba Al Hatmy of Salalah Port Services; Geoff O'Connor and Peter Kemp & all the staff of the Imperial War Museum (pages 44 and 46); the staff of the Public Records Office at Kew; Matt Jones of Boeing & FP7 (page 55); Fred Huntley, Terry Daly, Dawn Winn and Adrian Meredith of British Airways 44/45, 46/47, 46 inset; Bill Hunt of The Ministry of Defence photography department; Kim Hearn of the Quadrant Library of Flight International Magazine; Tony Kemp of W.J. Towell; Tushar Maheshwari of Khimji Ramdas; Anne Swain of the National Geographic Image Library, Washington (page 20, 27, 35 inset, 44 inset, 65, 85 inset, 97 inset, 102, 114/115, and 126); Gordon Barclay of the British Aerospace Library at Warton (page 14 inset); and finally to all the staff of the photographic archive and the map department of the Royal Geographic Society especially Clive Coward and Joanna Scudden (pages 2, 38, 95 inset, 102, 112 and 119 inset).

Retired members of the Royal Air Force, the British Army and the Royal Navy and other forces were particularly helpful in the making of this book; Sqn. Ldr. John Stewart-Smith, ex-No 1 (Fighter) Sqn (page 14 inset); the late Sqn. Ldr Ron Codrai, ex-No 625 Sqn. and No 156 Sqn., Pathfinder Force flying Lancasters; Dugold Cameron of No 84 Sqn; John Phillips; Bob & Jane McAllen; Jim Hood of No 206 Sqn.; Richard F. Smith of No 203 Sqn; Sqn. Ldr Tony Cunnane of the Red Arrows; Donnie Ray Ditty of the US Marines; Andy Durnsire (pages 6/7, 22 inset, 31, 53 inset, 51, 53 inset, 60/61, 62/63, 70/71, 72/73, 84, 89 inset, 90, 122/123, and 126 inset), Lou Lyddon of the Trucial Oman Scouts & Airwork (pages 1, 4, 76/77, 78/79, 84/85, 86 inset and front cover); Ted Marriott (page 55); Trevor Wilson; Mike Curtis (page 86 inset); John Miller of NSA; Dennis Pascoe; Ian Ord (page 52/53); Maurice Hynett; Kevin Smith, Duncan Donaldson, Baz Longhurst, Nick Mylne, Graham Jackson, Saud, Saif, Mansour, Said, Humaid, Dougal Lawton and the late Moh'd Moosa (who first landed with me at the tombs) serving with the Royal Flight of Oman; the late General Geoff Harcourt who gave me a first edition of "The Tribes Of Oman"; Hugh McCrae (page 54), Ray Deacon of No 37 Sqn; Sqn. Ldr Tom Sheppard, FRGS ARPS, former fighter pilot of No 208 Squadron; and finally, my thanks to the many undocumented members of the Royal Air Force who took photographs as part of their duties in the British Empire and Commonwealth so many years ago. The photographs by the Royal Air Force are British Crown copyright, and reproduced with the permission of the Controller of Her Britannic Majesty's Stationery Office. Special thanks to two artists; Christopher Southcombe, ex Royal Navy, for his impressive painting of the Sohar ship shown on the rear end paper and David Shepherd OBE FRCS GAVA, now an honoury member of the Royal Air Force Club for his continued support and his painting of the oryx on page 110 inset.

It was a pleasure to work with and receive the support and contributions of fellow photographers; Ozzie Newcombe (pages 86/87 & 92 inset), Sonia Carr, Robert and Irene Spikins (page 72 inset), Sue from SABCO, Ellie McCann, Mohammed Al Rashdi, Rodney Salm, Robert Baldwin, Iqbal Abdul Redha Sultan, Maurice Gent, Johan Palsson (pages 12 inset, 13, 32, 36, 64, 96 & 102 inset and 114) and Anju Visen Singh of Apex, Mark Mallett, the lovely lady from Salalah whose contact details I lost in our disastrous fire (page 112), Alan Pimm-Smith (page 32/33), Bruno Brokken, Dick Marston GCRS, Robert Richmond (page 78 inset, 112 inset), Susmit Dey (front end cover), Bob Spiteri, Paul Yule for several expeditions, Adil and Holly Bahwan; Chris & Heide Beal; Satish and Indra Chopra of Photocentre; Peter Metcalfe; Abdi Al Shawani of the Royal Stables; Mahmood Fakir Al Zadjali; Asad Raza and Hormaz Muncherjee, who provided the Zubair Tours vehicle for Paul Yule and I to reach the tombs; Pradeep Havaldar and Leo Fewtrell of OUA; Marycke Jongbloed and Roger Le Meister, Lamjed El Kefi (page 98 inset, 115 inset).

Our thanks to the following companies whose support and encouragement made the publication of this book possible; Isa Mohammed Al Hajri and Hafidh Al Busaidy of the Al Bhustan Palace Hotel; Nick Prest, Trevor Harrison and especially Mary Ann Griffiths of Alvis; Jeremy Bowen, Michael Wilson, Ali Al Khanjari and Tim Bingham of British Petroleum; Chris and Renate Hurndall of the Schooner "Charlotte Anne"; Anthony Wright and Sami Omar Al Zadjali of Oman International Bank; Abdul Rahaman Al Busaidy, Clive Raymond, Captain George Gilson, Nabil Zadjaly and Lorna King of Oman Air; Said Mahad, Dick Simmons, Robert Bray and Steve Martin of HSBC; Paul Dubeck of the Boeing Aircraft Company; and finally David Bath and especially Chris Grant, ex Royal Navy, ex Royal Oman Police Air Wing, of Westland Helicopters.

On a more personal note, I would like to express our gratitude to the following people, who continue to make a daily impact on my life, for

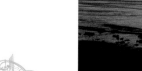

Dubai", my friend Frederick Secca-Blagg, my mother-in-law, Marjorie and my eldest son Marc for looking after the UK book distribution, Kerri for graduating from Sam Houston University with her Masters in Educational Psychology, my hearing impaired son, Nicholas, now **21**, who ably looks after the distribution of books in the USA while attending Lake City College, William, just **14** and six feet tall, for helping me with the layout and production of "Now & Then – New York" and finally to my wife, Christine, and my graphic designer, Nick Crawley, who together produced "Now & Then – Abu Dhabi".

their support, encouragement and patience: Robert & Simone for their continuous support in Dubai with their book "Now & Then –

Thanks to you all.
John J. Nowell *LRPS FRGS*,
Muscat, **2001**

Front End Paper: The "Tabula Asiae" map by Sebastian Munster was first printed in 1540. It was based on a map drawn in 150 AD by Ptolemy, the famous Greek astronomer and geographer, produced in Alexandria, Egypt.

Rear End Paper: This painting by Christopher Southcombe depicts the "Sohar Ship", a dhow built in 1970 on traditional lines. The photograph on the front cover shows this ship entering Canton Harbour having completed the entire journey on lanteen